Gifted & Talented in the Early Years

Education at SAGE

SAGE is a leading international publisher of journals, books, and electronic media for academic, educational, and professional markets.

Our education publishing includes:

- accessible and comprehensive texts for aspiring education professionals and practitioners looking to further their careers through continuing professional development

- inspirational advice and guidance for the classroom

- authoritative state of the art reference from the leading authors in the field

Find out more at: **www.sagepub.co.uk/education**

Gifted & Talented in the Early Years

Practical Activities for Children aged 3 to 6

Margaret Sutherland

2nd Edition

Los Angeles | London | New Delhi
Singapore | Washington DC

Los Angeles | London | New Delhi
Singapore | Washington DC

SAGE Publications Ltd
1 Oliver's Yard
55 City Road
London EC1Y 1SP

SAGE Publications Inc.
2455 Teller Road
Thousand Oaks, California 91320

SAGE Publications India Pvt Ltd
B 1/I 1 Mohan Cooperative Industrial Area
Mathura Road
New Delhi 110 044

SAGE Publications Asia-Pacific Pte Ltd
3 Church Street
#10-04 Samsung Hub
Singapore 049483

Commissioning editor: Jude Bowen
Editorial assistant: Miriam Davey
Project manager: Jeanette Graham
Assistant production editor: Thea Watson
Copyeditor: Rosemary Campbell
Proofreader: Isabel Kirkwood
Indexer: Margaret Sutherland
Marketing manager: Lorna Patkai
Cover design: Wendy Scott
Typeset by: C&M Digitals (P) Ltd, India
Printed in India by Replika Press Pvt Ltd

First edition published 2005

Second edition first published 2012

Library of Congress Control Number: 2011943227

British Library Cataloguing in Publication data

A catalogue record for this book is available from
the British Library

ISBN 978-1-4462-1108-3
ISBN 978-1-4462-1109-0 (pbk)

Contents

List of figures and tables

About the author

Margaret Sutherland is a lecturer in additional support needs at the University of Glasgow. She is the Director of The Scottish Network for Able Pupils and Deputy Director of the Centre for Research and Development in Adult and Lifelong Learning. She has 31 years' teaching experience in mainstream primary schools, behaviour support and latterly in higher education. She has written articles in the field of gifted and talented education and is author of *Developing the Gifted and Talented Young Learner* (SAGE, 2008). She speaks regularly at conferences, leads courses, workshops and seminars across the UK, and has worked with students and teachers in Korea, Tanzania, Malawi and Denmark.

Acknowledgements

My thanks go to Kirsteen who, as an inspirational five-year-old pupil in my class, set me off in the direction of gifted and talented education.

Thanks, too, go to the staff and children of Killermont Primary School and Nursery, Bearsden and Lenzie Primary School and Nursery, Lenzie. In particular I would like to thank Shona Mathieson, Susan May, Harji Kaur and Mairi Gillies for allowing me to visit their early years settings and for offering helpful and supportive comments at each stage of writing.

Advice and support were gratefully received from my colleagues and friends, Chris Smith and Niamh Stack, and from Jude Bowen at SAGE Publications.

Finally my thanks go to Andrew and Louis – the third dog to accompany me during the writing process – for 'putting up with me' as tensions rose and deadlines drew near.

The poem on page 126 is reproduced from *Global Citizenship: A Handbook for Primary Teaching*, 2002 with the permission of Oxfam GB, Oxfam House, John Smith Drive, Cowley, Oxford OX4 2JY, UK www.oxfam.org.uk/education, Oxfam GB does not necessarily endorse any text activities that accompany the materials.

Dedication

For all the children I have worked with – for those I discovered who were gifted and talented, and for the ones I missed because I didn't look in the right place or offer the right opportunities and challenges.

Preface

The importance of early education cannot be overestimated. A love of learning and a sense of excitement, purpose and creativity formed in the early years can go on to have lasting impact on the lives of young people. Opportunities offered in the early years can develop into lifelong passions, giving our world a diversity and richness that can only enhance and augment the lives of all. As someone working with young children you are in an ideal situation to offer these opportunities. It is a very privileged position to be in and one we need to take seriously if we are to help young children develop in a way that celebrates and cultivates their full range of abilities and aptitudes.

If you're reading this book then it is likely that you have in your care a child who is demonstrating abilities beyond what might be expected for their age. These children, sometimes referred to as 'tall poppies', will be doing things in your early years setting that often leave you standing in amazement – such as the three-year-old child who goes into the story corner and reads a book for themselves. There is no doubt that young children are often capable of more than we think. National initiatives in the UK (Early Intervention, Scotland; Foundation Stage, England and Wales) have helped to raise expectations among educators. Perhaps less well documented are the group of children who often receive the label 'gifted and talented'. It is the educational experiences of these children that this book will explore.

International (UN, 1989, 1994) and national (DfES, 1998, 2001; SEED, 2003; SOEID, 1994) initiatives have seen an ever-increasing move towards inclusive education. There is much debate as to what this term means and there are a plethora of books on the market that consider just this issue. For the purposes of this book, 'inclusive education' is taken to mean children learning together: learning from each other, from the adults around them and from their communities and families. The focus of this book will be to explore how we can meet the needs of the so-called 'tall poppies' mentioned above within an inclusive education framework.

The first chapter of this book sets out to explore how we might include gifted and talented individuals in our settings. It considers the labels we use to describe gifted and talented children and looks at how the adults' beliefs about intelligence will impact on what they do, say and look for in the early years setting. It challenges educators to think about the nature of intelligence and to think about inclusion in a new way.

Chapter 2 investigates the tricky area of identification. It suggests practical ways of identifying young gifted and talented learners – interview questions, observation sheets and tracking sheets are suggested as ways of building up an 'holistic picture' of a child and their abilities. It considers how culture, history and educational experiences influence responses to gifted education and highlights the common issues countries across the globe grapple with when providing for gifted and talented children.

Chapter 3 considers four curriculum areas – physical movement/motor development, music, language and mathematics – and offers some suggestions as to what may be advanced responses to common early years activities and resources in these areas.

The next four chapters, Chapters 4–7, consider each individual curricular area and contain ideas for challenging activities. The activity sheets can be used as they appear or can be adapted and developed to suit individual settings. These chapters may be 'dipped in and out of' as a particular need in a particular curricular area arises.

The final chapter pulls together the thoughts and ideas from throughout the book and links these to common practice found in early years settings. It highlights the need to challenge our gifted and talented children and to ensure that we offer challenging learning opportunities for all.

You will see six icons appearing throughout the book:

 This icon indicates that there are some key points that early educators should bear in mind when working with young gifted and talented learners.

 This icon suggests some points for staff to reflect on when there are things that practitioners and settings need to think about when providing for gifted and talented children.

 This icon shows where there are useful activities for practitioners to try.

 This icon means you can photocopy these pages.

 These icons indicate some further sources of information and offer some suggestions to get you started.

 This icon appears at the end of chapters to provide an overview of the key points.

1

Including the gifted and talented in the early years

Some key points about the education of gifted and talented learners will be made in this chapter.

> • **Adopting an inclusive approach to learning is helpful to young gifted and talented learners.**
>
> • **Current learning theory and changes in the way we think about learning, ability and intelligence offer an opportunity to ensure all abilities are being challenged and celebrated.**
>
> • **Labels for gifted and talented learners, while useful, can also be a hindrance. We need to focus on what the labels mean and try to come to some shared understandings about the terms used.**
>
> • **Intelligence is difficult to define. It is our beliefs about intelligence that will influence our view of children in the early years setting and impact on individuals' self-beliefs or mindsets.**

Who are the gifted and talented in your early years setting?

I wonder what picture you have in your mind of a child who is gifted and talented? Often we conjure up images of a round-faced kid with freckles and glasses. He/she always answers questions correctly and is often to be found on his/her own, usually doing science experiments. He/she is sometimes known as 'the little professor'. Or perhaps it is the virtuoso violin player who happens to be four years old. He/she spends hours practising almost to the exclusion of everything else; he/she is quietly spoken and is good at mathematics as well. This kind of stereotyping, while common, is not helpful, particularly if we're considering the education of young gifted and talented children within an inclusive education framework. For many, these narrow views of who the gifted and talented are will go on to shape and influence what they do with young children in their care.

- What does it mean to be gifted and talented in your setting?
- How might your views on gifted and talented children influence practice in your setting?
- What kinds of things do children do in your setting that make you say 'wow!'?

The early years setting should be an exciting place to be for all children. It is also the ideal place to discuss the education of gifted and talented children. Through the provision of appropriate activities and interaction with adults, the setting should offer young children the opportunity to:

- discover what they are interested in

- discover what they can do

- develop relationships with others (adults and children)

- learn to work alongside others (adults and children)

- take risks.

Early years settings, by their very nature, are often considered to be inclusive in the care and education of young children. The structure and practice within early years settings would seem to allow for the adoption of an inclusive approach to learning. For one thing, a play-centred curriculum allows for a child-centred approach: children drive the learning process. This is not to say that there is no structure and that goals are not set, it's just that learning and development are seen as important and complementary, and the emphasis is not simply on targets and results. The child focus of staff and the flexible structure within early years allow for the development of inclusive practices.

Inclusion in the early years setting

Inclusion is an international concept stemming from the International Declaration on the Rights of the Child (UN, 1989). Inclusion can be looked at from two perspectives:

1   the current reality for particular groups of individuals for whom exclusion has been and continues to be the norm; and

2   an alternative concept of inclusion which encompasses all members of society rather than just a few.

In education the inclusion debate is often narrowed into a discussion about children who present with difficulties and where to educate them – in mainstream school or special schools? The world of gifted education has not been immune to this debate. Many programmes, centres and summer schools offer gifted individuals special pull-out programmes and opportunities. Blogs and websites discuss the relative merits of 'schools for the gifted'. Traditionally in the UK education systems we have excluded 'children that don't fit' – those with physical impairment, behaviour difficulties, learning difficulties and yes … even the gifted and talented. When we see a child doing something that is unusual in some way we often seek to identify what it is that is different and then we go about finding a label to explain this difference. We may even try to 'fix' the difference, just so they're 'normal'. While young children may react non-judgmentally to those who are different they are nonetheless developing an awareness of difference which may result in prejudices emerging and so it is important that educators think about encouraging awareness of, and positive attitudes to, diversity and difference within the setting. A shared view of inclusion does not exist at present, however, I would suggest that inclusion is about all individuals in society and as such assumes a 'whole' in which everyone has an equivalent part.

Feeling included

Feeling included, and of course the opposite, excluded, are feelings we will all have had from time to time. Consider the following example told to my colleague:

> John found it really awkward taking Josie to playgroup. He was the only father in the area who had made the decision to stay at home and look after his children. He was never part of the incidental chat the women took part in and always felt out of things on the nursery trips. Equally he felt he had less and less in common with male friends. He had commented that if only there were less stereotypical images of who looks after children things might be better.

- Can you think of a time when you felt excluded?
- How did it make you feel?
- What was the impact of these feelings on your behaviour?
- What was the impact of these feelings on your self-esteem and self-worth?
- What would have helped you to feel more included?

Gifted and talented children will sometimes feel excluded from the games their peers play. Sometimes staff interpret this as the gifted child having poor interpersonal skills and being immature. However this is not as simple as it might first appear. Let's look at this from the gifted child's perspective.

A group of children are playing in the house corner. The children have taken on traditional roles and are engaged in a make-believe game. The 'baby' in the 'family' is ill and is in bed. The gifted child approaches and the following happens:

Gifted child: *Can I play?*

Mum: *OK.*

Gifted child: *Can I be the doctor? I think I know what's wrong with the baby.*

Mum:	*No.*
Gifted child:	*But I think I can make her better.*
Mum:	*She's got a cold.*
Gifted child:	*No she hasn't, I think she's got malaria. You get that when a female mosquito bites you. What are the symptoms? Has she been in the tropics?*
Mum:	*She's got a cold.*
Gifted child:	*I know how you make malaria better. She needs to come to hospital and she'll need to get chloroquine, mefloquine, or quinine. Can I be the doctor?*
Mum:	*No. She's got a cold. She's not got your fancy illness. You can be the dog.*

The gifted child walks away muttering under their breath saying *I know how to make her better.*

There are several things happening here but on a basic level the gifted child has been excluded from the game. There may be several reasons for this but we will look at two related issues:

1   The game is already established and the existing group do not want another person to join.

2   The gifted child wants to develop the plot using their knowledge of real-life issues which the rest have no experience of or interest in.

The first reason relates to group dynamics and this may or may not have anything to do with the child being gifted per se. The 'mother' designates a role for the gifted child that 'fits' with the existing story. Joining in on that basis means play can continue. The second reason, while it relates not only to gifted children, does throw up some particularly interesting issues for gifted children. Gifted children will often have in-depth knowledge about a subject or subjects. They can be good at connecting that knowledge to different situations. They can also make up complex plots and story lines in their heads. Their age peers may just not understand what they are talking about and so they set about excluding them from the game, thus re-affirming existing group dynamics. In the scenario above the gifted child walks away but another outcome could be that the gifted child sets their complex plot aside and, in this case, would get down on all fours and start to bark. Gifted children can choose to be excluded from play and maintain the complex plot in their head or they can give up their complex plot in order to conform to the story and join the group. While on one level they may feel more included by 'joining in', as educators, we should be concerned if this happens on a regular basis. Children might stop sharing those complex plots; they may even begin to stop the elaborate thought processes – why bother if no one is interested? If this happens how will we know that they were and are capable of this higher level thinking? This is one example related to play but this may repeat itself in a variety of situations within the setting. Educators need to use such opportunities to increase young children's willingness to be inclusive of those who are different to themselves.

- How are difference and diversity celebrated in your setting?
- How do educators encourage children to be accepting of difference within the setting?
- In what ways do educators ensure that all children are valued within the setting?
- In what ways does the setting ensure that young gifted children are included appropriately in activities?

A danger when early years settings start to identify gifted and talented learners is that they lose what makes the early years setting experience unique and child-centred, and instead start to adopt the formal approaches offered in schools. While this may be appropriate for some, it will not be appropriate for all. That young gifted and talented learners need to be challenged is not debatable; how we do this perhaps requires further discussion. For the purposes of this book, inclusive education is taken to mean children learning together: learning from each other, from adults around them and from their communities and families. In this way, it is argued, gifted and talented learners can be:

- challenged appropriately

- seen as valuable members of the learning community

- have their gifts and talents recognised and celebrated within an inclusive setting.

So what do we know about learning that will help us to do this?

Learning in the early years setting

Much has been written about learning and how we learn. Advances in science and medicine, for example, mean we now know much more than we did in the past about how our brain functions and the impact that this has on learning. However, this knowledge has not always changed what we do as educators.

The point of looking at theory is that it offers vital insights into the day-to-day practice of learners, educators and settings, but often theory is overlooked in the busy day-to-day organising and planning of a setting and so is disregarded. A well-known theorist and academic wrote:

> An eminent professor who has researched and lectured on education for years is persuaded by one of his students to go out to schools and see good practice. On the way back in the car the professor is very quiet and the student asks him what he made of his day. 'Well,' replied the professor, 'I was just wondering if it would all work in theory'. (Ainscow, 1998: 7)

This anecdote highlights the false and unnecessary division between theory and practice. Theory without practice is useless, practice without theory is dangerous.

A number of theories have developed about learning, intelligence and ability. Any theory reflects a 'moment' in time. Theories come and go and collapse in on themselves when society changes. We learn new things that suggest the theory needs to change, adapt or be modified. This can give the impression that we are going round in circles. There is also a tendency to throw out everything we've been doing in the past, because it is somehow viewed as bad and outdated, in the naive belief that all the so-called new ideas will somehow be better and provide the answers.

The activities in this book emerge from a particular paradigm or worldview. A paradigm is described by Lewis (1998) as an interconnecting set of assumptions, values and methodologies that are accepted as self-evident. Lots of theories and approaches can be part of the same paradigm because they share the same world view. Thus the main theories reflected in this book belong to the social constructivist approach to learning and teaching and are part of what Poplin (1988) calls the new paradigm. New ways of looking at gifted and talented education and at early years education are being explored (Lenz Taguchi, 2010; Ziegler, 2005) and also call for a paradigm shift. The common theme across these new paradigms is that we need to change our thinking in relation to learning and think not about how we identify more people within the system but think about how we transform the system. This book is therefore concerned with how we can best create learning opportunities for young children that will allow their abilities to emerge and be nurtured.

As part of this new paradigm a social constructivist approach tells us there are some key things we know about learning that are important and will maximise learning for all learners:

- Learning is a social activity.

- Children learn best from collaborative activities – but we need to carefully craft the experiences.

- Experiences gained outside of the early years setting should be linked to the learning taking place in the early years setting.

- Learning in early years settings should be contextualised and not divorced from real-world experiences.

Taking these points into account, there are a number of core principles that underpin good learning experiences for all children. Bearing in mind this includes those who are gifted and talented, some principles might be:

- All children have a right to an education that is appropriately challenging and takes account of individual needs.

- Each person has a unique profile across a wide range of abilities that should be recognised, enhanced and valued equally.

- Recognition of an individual's ability profile is only possible in partnership with parents and other significant individuals in that person's life.

- Appropriate challenge must be provided at all points on an individual's ability profile.

- The key to recognition of an individual's abilities lies with the provision of appropriately challenging opportunities.

- Errors are critical to the learning process, thus appropriately challenging opportunities may require challenges that take the individual to the point of failure. This is only possible, however, within an ethos where it is safe to fail.

- An inclusive education system is the most supportive framework for offering opportunities to prevent underachievement and provide appropriate challenge across the ability range.

(Scottish Network for Able Pupils, 2004)

These principles form the framework for learning discussed in subsequent chapters, and if adopted would offer a framework for addressing the needs of gifted and talented learners.

Labels in an early years setting

We like the world to make sense and to help us we often label things. So the young child who learns the word 'bath' refers to all water as 'bath'. This gives us a sense of order and comfort. As adults we still seek to label things in order to categorise them and for ease of explanation. In the case of young gifted and talented children, there are a plethora of labels used to describe them. Indeed, these labels are often attributed to all children who show particular aptitude.

Here are just some of the more common words and phrases used in the UK:

- Smart
- Bright
- Precocious
- Clever
- Switched on
- Bright as a button
- Smart cookie

- Bright spark
- Clever clogs
- High achiever
- More able
- Special aptitude
- Gifted
- Talented

Each one of these words or phrases brings with it 'baggage' – particular connotations and meanings. How adults view children's abilities will often depend on the adult's view of intelligence; this in turn will influence their choice of description and indeed will influence whether the adult thinks that the ability being demonstrated is worthwhile and worthy of a label in the first place. Let's unpack these labels a little and see what lies behind them.

Traditionally in the UK we have tended to equate intelligence with mathematical and linguistic aptitude. Abilities that fall outside these domains are often not recognised. Many of the labels listed above are used to describe children who have shown aptitude in mathematics and language. So you will hear the four-year-old who can read being described as 'a real bright spark'. Likewise, children who have ability in mathematics will often be described as 'gifted' or 'a smart cookie'. Because words and phrases mean different things to different people, we can end up with staff in an early years setting all using the same word or words but actually talking about different things. The danger is not in the fact that we all use different words to describe abilities and children, it is that we assign different values and meaning to different words. Similarly, if all staff in the early years setting hold a very narrow view of what it is to be intelligent, then abilities that lie outside the narrow definition are unlikely to be recognised or challenged.

While labels can sometimes be helpful they can also cause problems. For example:

- we don't all use the same words to describe the same abilities

- labels can set up misleading expectations – for children, parents and staff

- people look no further than the label

- they lead to a child only being challenged in what they are already good at

- they might be limiting and disguise the child's other abilities.

Therefore it might be more beneficial to focus on what lies behind these labels. If we can start to come to some kind of shared understanding as to what we think being gifted and talented might mean, then we can start to think about what we value and how we can challenge the abilities that the children in our care demonstrate. In other words, let's not agonise over what label we assign, but instead let's engage in discussion about what the words actually mean to us and what they mean for learning. In this way we do not become caught up with the comparative notions of giftedness where we say 'he/she is gifted in my setting but not in the one down the road' but instead we focus on what the children are doing and how we might move their learning forward.

- Decide what you mean by intelligence.

- Agree whether intelligence is about mathematics and language only or whether it includes other areas of the curriculum.

- Agree on what words/labels you will use to describe children who are displaying particular abilities in the areas you decide on.

What is intelligence?

Just what does it mean to be intelligent? For years we have tried to describe what being intelligent means, but Colman (1987) suggests that there is no precise definition of intelligence that would satisfy all psychologists and points out that dictionary definitions are of little help.

> The *Oxford English Dictionary* lists twelve definitions of 'intelligence'; but it also lists eight definitions of 'definition' and no fewer than 114 definitions of 'of'. What a muddle! (1987: 17)

No one is sure exactly what intelligence is although there are lots of different views. These views are, generally, encapsulated in models that seek to illustrate the different theories that exist. Intelligence is often measured by standardised tests that the child has taken, from which their IQ is established. To suggest that a certain percentage of children are 'intelligent' by reference to a single test score is neither helpful to the identification procedure nor to selecting the most effective form of provision (Koshy and Casey, 1997). The test may have been standardised on a population that was vastly different from the one to which the child being tested belongs. Not only is the population different, but also cultural differences may be significant to the outcome of the test. Neither do such tests take account of creativity or divergent thinking – abilities which a gifted and talented child will often demonstrate. David George (1997) suggests that while an IQ test may allow the identification of some children with certain abilities, it may be more to do with the fact that these children:

> perform well in academic subjects ... are persistent, respond well to instruction, have good study skills ... process information quickly, have better memories, have greater accuracy and are good at abstract thinking. (George, 1997: 37)

In other words, they're good at passing tests!

This still leaves us with our original question – what does it mean to be intelligent? The work of Howard Gardner (1983) in the USA encouraged us to think differently about intelligence. He suggested that intelligence is not just about maths and language but includes a much wider range of abilities. He also argued we all have all of them to a greater or lesser degree and they are not hierarchical. Gardner's list includes:

- linguistic intelligence (word smart)

- mathematical intelligence (logic smart)

- interpersonal intelligence (people smart)

- naturalist intelligence (nature smart)

- visual-spatial intelligence (picture smart)

- musical intelligence (music smart)

- bodily kinaesthetic intelligence (body smart)

- intrapersonal intelligence (self smart)

- existential intelligence (wonder smart).

What would young children be doing if they were demonstrating abilities in these areas? Table 1.1 gives some examples.

Table 1.1 Abilities associated with different intelligences

Intelligence	Evidence	Famous people
Linguistic (word smart)	• Tells stories and jokes • Good memory for names, dates, etc. • Enjoys word games • Likes tongue twisters • Has a good vocabulary • Communicates well	• Shakespeare • Hemingway • J.K. Rowling • Agatha Christie • Elizabeth Barrett Browning
Logical/mathematical (number smart)	• Plays chess and strategy games • Understands cause and effect • Asks questions about how things work • Can do arithmetic in their heads quickly	• Archimedes • Sir Isaac Newton • Einstein
Interpersonal (people smart)	• Enjoys being with peers • A natural leader • Offers advice to friends • Has close friends • Others want to be their friend	• Oprah Winfrey • Abraham Lincoln • Gandhi • Martin Luther King
Naturalist (nature smart)	• Enjoys learning about animals or nature • An interest in biology, zoology, geology, astronomy • Aware of the environment • Categorises easily • Likes beauty and the outside world	• Galileo • Jacques Cousteau • Dian Fossey
Visual/spatial (picture smart)	• Reads maps, charts and diagrams easily • Enjoys puzzles, jigsaws, I spy • Builds 3-dimensional constructions • Draws in advance of age • Understands pictures more than words	• Michelangelo • Picasso • Steven Spielberg • Monet
Musical (music smart)	• Knows when music is 'off key' • Remembers the tune to a song • Sings well • Can keep the rhythm • Imitates others easily • Plays an instrument	• Mozart • Beethoven • Scott Joplin • John Lennon
Bodily kinaesthetic (body smart)	• Good at sports • Can mimic gestures • Good fine-motor skills • Likes plasticine, clay and hands on art activities • Has difficulty sitting still • Very active	• Tiger Woods • Marcel Marceau • David Beckham • Wayne Rooney

Intelligence	Evidence	Famous people
Intrapersonal (self smart)	• Independent • Plays well alone • Aware of strengths/weaknesses • Can express how they are feeling • Learns from mistakes	• Joan of Arc • Sir Edmund Hillary • Neil Armstrong • Christopher Columbus
Existential (wonder smart)	• Asks big questions about life/death • Asks questions about other planets • Appears to be fully aware of the cosmos • Asks life's larger questions	• Aristotle • Confucius • Einstein • Plato • Socrates

This wider approach to intelligence links well with existing work in the early years setting and allows for an holistic or whole-person approach to development and the recognition of abilities. However, in spite of this wider approach it is often children who display abilities in mathematics (logic smart) and language (word smart) that are identified.

An American psychologist called Carol Dweck (1999) has considered theories of intelligence. She has split these into two broad categories – entity theory of intelligence and incremental theory of intelligence.

Holding an **entity view of intelligence** will mean believing a person possesses a specific amount of intelligence and nothing you or they can do will change that amount. In other words:

- it's fixed

- you've only got so much of it

- there's not much you can do about how much you've got

- there's nothing you can do as the educator to increase the amount they've got.

If you hold this belief you are likely to say the following things:

Holding an **incremental view of intelligence** will mean believing that intelligence is not an 'entity' that resides within a person but is something that can be developed through learning. In other words:

- it can change

- you can become more intelligent

- the more you learn, the more you can learn

- the educator can work with the person so they become more intelligent.

If you hold this belief you are likely to say the following things:

Dweck uses these two categories – entity and incremental – to explain people's understanding of, and beliefs about, intelligence. It is these beliefs about intelligence that will influence our expectations of children and our approaches to working with children.

These two very different beliefs will result in very different behaviours within individuals. For example, Dweck suggests the following:

Learning is fixed (entity)	Learning can change (incremental)
worry about how much fixed intelligence they have	believe everyone with effort and guidance can increase their intellectual abilities
need to look and feel like they have enough 'intelligence'	need to learn
need to look smart and need to out-perform others	sacrifice opportunities to look smart in favour of opportunities to learn something new
need easy successes	thrive on challenge

(Dweck, 1999: p. 3)

These beliefs about intelligence are closely linked to what Dweck calls 'goal achievement' (Dweck, 1999). By this she means that if you hold a fixed view of intelligence then it will be performance goals that will be important to you because you need to show just how clever and smart you are. In contrast, if you possess an incremental view of intelligence then you will be concerned with becoming smarter, and so learning goals will be more important to you.

Dweck argues that your belief about intelligence greatly influences how you approach tasks. Those who believed intelligence was fixed opted for easier tasks that would make them look smart, and those who thought it could change sought out interesting, challenging tasks that would take forward their learning.

Young children's ideas about intelligence

Often children arrive in the early years setting with definite views about themselves and their abilities. How often have you heard the statement 'I can't do difficult jigsaws, only easy ones'? There could be a number of reasons for this type of response.

At one time people believed that young children didn't really understand the concept of intelligence. When a young child 'failed' at a task it was believed that this failure didn't automatically lead to pessimistic feelings about themselves and their abilities, as it seemed to in older children. However, the work of Dweck and others challenged this idea.

Dweck suggests that young children are not so much interested in intelligence; this, she argues, develops as the child becomes older. Rather, children are concerned with ideas about 'goodness' and 'badness'. This can be seen in the early years setting and in life generally as young children explore and often challenge the rules and possibilities that are set before them. Interaction with and reaction from family members, peers and adults in the early years setting all help the young child to begin to build up a picture of themselves. Perhaps that's where the statement about the jigsaws comes from. Dweck argues that vulnerable young children 'feel they are bad when they encounter failure or criticism. And – just like older children with intelligence – they think that badness is a stable trait' (Dweck, 1999: 97). If young children grow up believing that mistakes and failure are bad and it therefore makes them feel bad, then it is likely that they will spend much of their time avoiding making mistakes. This is not helpful if we accept that mistakes are a vital part of the learning process. There is also evidence to suggest that if they accept that this 'badness' or 'failure' is innate, in other words fixed, then they believe there's nothing they can do about it. When later these ideas of 'goodness' and 'badness' or 'failure' and 'success' are transported into school and academic life it is perhaps hardly surprising that we find children who are desperate to show you how clever or smart they are. They need you to know 'I'm not stupid'. From an early age learners start to evaluate their own abilities and so build up a personal theory relating to intelligence. Information that helps them to do this comes from three sources:

- through comparison with others

- through feedback from significant others

- through interactions within their own particular contexts.

(McLean, 2003)

Dweck argues that these ideas of 'goodness' and 'badness' feed into mindsets. A mindset is another way of talking about belief in yourself. Thus, along with views about intelligence being fixed or incremental, children build up one of two mindsets – a fixed mindset or a growth mindset. The good news is that we can influence young children's views of themselves so they become interested in learning. A growth mindset will support children during difficult times in their lives. How we influence children's views will depend on our own beliefs about intelligence.

To influence children's views about themselves in a positive way, educators need to:

- believe that intelligence is not fixed

- acknowledge that genetics plays a part but not 'write children off' because of who their parents are

- encourage young children to make mistakes and learn from them

- praise the amount of effort a child puts into an activity.

Fixed or changeable? What does this mean for the early years setting?

So what does all this mean for our gifted and talented learners, and us as adults, working in the early years setting? Two things are important here in relation to your work in the early years setting:

1   Your view of intelligence will influence how you view children in the early years setting.

2   You can influence children's views about intelligence and their ideas about their own intelligence.

Let's think for a minute about how the two different theoretical approaches/views might manifest themselves in everyday life in the early years setting.

A person with a fixed view of intelligence is likely to say the following:

Robin is a very bright boy.
He's very good at numbers. He always
gets all the number activities right first time.
He can be a bit of a show-off actually.
Of course his dad is a joiner, he's very good at
numbers, and his big sister was good too,
it runs in the family.

A person who thinks intelligence can change is likely to comment:

Robin loves numbers, works very hard at number activites and works out number puzzles quickly. He needs a challenge as often the number activities are simple for him. His big sister liked numbers too and his dad's a joiner, perhaps they help him at home.

These two slightly different approaches are underpinned by divergent philosophies and if Robin is the recipient of one approach over the other it is likely to result in Robin approaching numbers in a particular way.

In our first scenario the adult believes this ability in mathematics is innate and inherited. There is an assumption that Robin is naturally good with numbers and that in fact he's so good he shows off about it. Robin will learn from this that:

- your abilities are not always appreciated and are perhaps something you should keep quiet about

- he should always find number activities easy.

Over time staff may assume that Robin will be good at number activities. They may:

- try to catch him out with something in order to show him he 'doesn't know it all', or

- be pleased when he finds a particular number task difficult and challenging.

In the second scenario the staff member believes that Robin puts considerable effort into his number tasks and this effort may occur in the early years setting or at home with siblings. Either way, the staff member does not suggest that this ability in number just happens. They also acknowledge that Robin requires challenge, suggesting that number tasks should not always come easily. Robin will learn that effort is expected and that it is this effort that helps him to succeed at numbers.

Early years practitioners will:

- offer support and strategies when tasks are difficult

- encourage him to adopt new number strategies and work alongside others.

That Robin undoubtedly has a propensity towards numbers is not being denied here, but the crucial difference between this view and the view outlined previously is that this ability is developing because of support, challenging activities and effort on Robin's part and not simply because he has some predisposition to mathematics.

How we react to children will also be influenced by our underlying beliefs and these may be inadvertently transferred to the child. While a response such as 'Well done, you've got these all right. You're really clever' may seem to be supportive, there is evidence to suggest that over time when it is the child we praise, suggesting that there is some innate, inherent ability, it will lead the child to assume he or she is 'clever'. When they meet difficulty and failure they will assume they can't do the task because they are not clever enough. After all, they have always been clever in the past – hasn't the early years setting worker always told them that? Comments such as 'You've tried really hard there. Well done', on the other hand, will mean that when meeting with failure it is not their intelligence or ability that is being called into question but perhaps it is just a different way of approaching the task that is required. After all, they have always tried really hard in the past – hasn't the early years setting worker always told them that?

These two simple illustrations begin to demonstrate how over time our beliefs and reactions will impact on a child and will contribute towards their view or mindset of themselves either as individuals who can learn more and go on learning or as individuals who have learned as much as they are capable of learning.

The early years setting that considers intelligence to be multifaceted and something that can be developed will promote the identification of gifted and talented children in a broader and more inclusive way.

 Summing up

Some key points about the education of gifted and talented learners have been made in this chapter.

- By and large, early years settings adopt an inclusive approach to learning that is helpful to young gifted and talented learners.
- Current learning theory and new ways of thinking about learning, intelligence and ability offer an opportunity to ensure all abilities are being challenged and celebrated.
- Labels for gifted and talented learners, while useful, can also be a hindrance. We need to focus on what the labels mean and try to come to some shared understandings about the terms used.
- Intelligence is difficult to define. It is our beliefs about intelligence that will influence our view of children in the early years setting and impact on individuals' self-beliefs or mindsets.

Useful websites

Carol Dweck: https://www.stanford.edu/dept/psychology/cgi-bin/drupalm/cdweck Carol Dweck's personal webpage has links to a number of interesting papers about self-belief, mindsets, intelligence, etc.

Carol Dweck: http://www.carol-dweck.co.uk/uploads/643_Dweck%20UK%20Slides% 20June%202010.pdf This webpage contains slides that explain more about mindsets.

Further reading

Porter, L. (2005) *Gifted Young Children: A Guide for Teachers and Parents.* Maidenhead: Open University Press.

Sutherland, M. (2008) *Developing the Gifted and Talented Young Learner.* London: SAGE Publications.

Yelland, N. (2010) *Contemporary Perspectives on Early Childhood Education.* Maidenhead: Open University Press.

2

Identification

Some key points about the identification of gifted and talented learners will be made in this chapter.

- **Labels for children are not always necessary, but challenging learning experiences are.**
- **Assessment should be about learning, not plugging gaps in knowledge and skills.**
- **We need to build up the whole picture of the child's abilities and interests.**
- **The information we gather can help us to plan next steps and challenging learning experiences.**
- **Culture plays a part in the learning process.**
- **There are common issues relating to gifted education being discussed internationally.**

To label or not to label?

People working in early years settings must avoid falling into the trap of thinking that they can easily identify the gifted and talented simply because children possess particular stereotypical dispositions. For example, children are often identified as being gifted and talented if they are:

- articulate
- confident
- reading well and early
- born during September to December
- mature
- vivacious
- charismatic

or have

- 'bright' elder siblings

- a good general knowledge

- good fine and gross motor skills.

Contrast this with children who:

- are quiet and withdrawn

- struggle with words

- have poor fine and gross motor skills

- have a summer birthday

- are dishevelled

- are unappealing

- have English as a second language

- are 'badly' behaved.

These children are less likely to be immediately considered to be gifted and talented. Discovery of abilities, therefore, must be the focus of the early years setting. Offering a wide and varied range of opportunities to all will allow young children to explore and uncover the abilities they possess. The early years setting would do well to concentrate on maximising opportunities for learning. It is this that will allow gifted and talented learners to blossom and be identified, rather than some predetermined set of assumptions.

However, if, as was suggested in Chapter 1, you've arrived at a working definition of what it means to be gifted and talented, you will now be keen to find out how many of the children you work with might have gifts and/or talents that need to be challenged and developed. So what do we do? The easy answer is identify them. However, the identification of gifted and talented children is a thorny subject. If it were as simple as ticking boxes on a checklist we wouldn't need chapters on identification. Since we are talking about human beings and attributes, it follows that neat checklists will only go some way to helping us identify children and their abilities. But perhaps there is an even more fundamental question we need to be asking ourselves – if, as I have suggested previously, labelling can be dangerous as well as helpful, then should we be seeking to identify children in the early years setting as gifted and talented at all?

There is an anxiety on the part of educators and parents that labelling a child as gifted and talented at an early age may result in the following:

- being isolated from their peers (Gross, 1993)

- once labelled, 'hot-housing' may occur, during which time young children may 'switch off' their special talent or ability (Mares, 1991)

- over the years other children may 'catch up' with the 'gifted and talented' children and so while still 'very good', they no longer merit the label 'gifted and talented'.

The effect of all this on children may be detrimental to learning in the long term. Parents too may feel 'under pressure' or confused. While care must be taken to avoid such scenarios, it should not be at the expense of providing appropriate and challenging activities for young children. Concern can lead to inactivity. I would suggest that we should not worry too much about assigning a label, but instead should gather information about the child that allows us to offer appropriate challenging learning experiences. In other words, let's improve assessment, which will allow us to identify and cater appropriately for all children.

Assessment for learning

Quality pre-school experiences enhance a child's learning and development, and early childhood is a critical time for such development (Thurtle, 1997). If doing nothing is an unacceptable option, what should we be doing? In many ways identification is inextricably linked to assessment. Many people spend huge amounts of time checking to see that children have 'learned' a predetermined set of skills that will ensure they make a good start at 'formal' school. By doing this, educators can identify the gaps that exist and seek to plug these through extra practice, homework and one-to-one tuition. The effect of this kind of assessment on learning and individuals is neatly described in a story told to me by a nursery teacher:

> It's June in the nursery and for the past week and a half I have spent my time walking around with a red clipboard 'testing' children, particularly in mathematics and language, recording results and completing forms for the 'big' school. I walked over to a table where a nursery nurse and four children were working on an activity. I was in fact going to ask the nursery nurse if she had watched a particular programme on TV the night before. On approaching the table with my red clipboard one of the children turned to look at me. On seeing the red clipboard he looked up into my face and said confidently 'It's red and it's a triangle'. (Nursery teacher)

Perhaps some of the traditional forms of assessment that exist are unhelpful. While this true story probably brought a smile to your face, it strikes me as a sad indictment of our education systems if that is the first reaction of a four-year-old to the approach of an adult in the early years setting.

However, assessment can be quite different. It is more helpful to find out what children can learn with help and support rather than simply testing what they have already learned. Assessment that supports the learning process can help to challenge gifted and talented learners, extending their learning rather than merely giving them more of something they are already good at. Indeed, a new approach to the assessment of all children will benefit those who are gifted and talented and help us to identify emerging abilities. It will also help us to meet the requirements expected of us by our various education systems.

Margaret Carr (2001) suggests that we need to rethink assessment. We need to focus on learning instead of the idea that there is a predetermined set of skills or that there is predetermined knowledge that a child must possess. The old style of assessment she has called a 'folk model' of assessment. In other words, it is a set of beliefs about assessment that have grown and developed over the years with no one challenging them or questioning the rationale for them. She suggests we need to move towards an 'alternative model' of assessment where the learners' understanding is arrived at by collaboration between the adult and the learner (see Table 2.1).

Table 2.1 Assumption in two models of assessment: a folk model and an alternative

Assumptions about	Folk model of assessment	An alternative model of assessment
Purpose	To check against a shortlist of skills that describe 'competence' at school entry	To enhance learning
Outcome of interest	Fragmented and context-free school-oriented skills	Learning dispositions
Focus of intervention	Deficit, gap-filling, is foregrounded	Credit, disposition enhancing, is foregrounded
Validity	Objective observation	Interpreted observations, discussions and agreements
Progress	Hierarchies of skills	Increasingly complex participation
Procedures	Checklists	Learning stories
Value to practitioners	Surveillance by external agencies	For communicating with four audiences: children, families, other staff and self (the practitioner)

Reprinted by permission of SAGE Publications Ltd from Margaret Carr, *Assessment in Early Childhood Settings*, © Margaret Carr 2001

In the folk model the following may happen. Staff in the early years setting draw up a checklist of predetermined skills that children will undertake. Successful completion of these tasks will indicate that a child is ready to move on to the next task or is ready to start 'formal' school, etc. These tasks are likely to be familiar to you and might include:

- colouring in within the lines (i.e. 'neatly')

- using scissors (without looking as though they might stab themselves or someone else)

- writing their name independently (e.g. on their art work)

- recognising numbers (e.g. from environmental print)

- reciting the numbers 1–20 and beyond

- knowing some letter and sound names (e.g. 'What sound does your name begin with?')

- knowing which way to hold a book (when in the library corner)

- knowing how to turn over the pages of a book

- knowing that print reads from left to right.

These tasks may be explicitly taught and they will almost certainly be tested. There will be an assumption that children must be able to complete these tasks with ease before moving on to other skills. Indeed there will be an assumption that learning will be difficult and may even be hindered if a child is unable to complete these apparently basic and crucial skills. These tasks can be neatly ticked off on a list, the information can be passed on to formal school and there may be assumptions that these children will 'do well' as they progress through the education system. I am not arguing here that these 'skills' are not important; however, I am saying that we cannot look at them in isolation, we cannot say that a child who is proficient at these things is necessarily gifted and talented, and we cannot say they will undoubtedly 'do well'.

How, then, do we make these changes to assessment? In the 'alternative model' of assessment the following may occur. Staff in the early years setting will:

- find out what children already know, understand and can do

- discuss with children what the learning goals are for the activity

- discuss with children what they have done well and what they need to work on, and what they put their progress down to

- allow children to experiment with resources

- look for children who persist with a task

- encourage children to express points of view and emotions.

Children who demonstrate these abilities may also score very well on our previous list, but being proficient in the dispositions in the alternative model is, in the longer term, more beneficial as the child enters formal school. These dispositions are a firm grounding for meaningful lifelong learning and not simply a list of tasks proving they are skilled at 'hoop jumping'. Yet, these kinds of 'dispositions' do not lend themselves to an accountability-based approach to learning. They don't fit neatly into a checklist or tick-box culture. However, they are extremely important if we believe that learning is not about a single end point, but rather a multiplicity of end points. In other words, end points are made up of a number of dispositions with no one factor being more important than another – the *process* is as important as the *product*. If it is important to staff and parents that things are neat, tidy, ordered and as near perfect as possible, then this suggested change of emphasis from 'product to process' may well be difficult. Full explanations of the shift in emphasis in assessment should be given to all before embarking on such a change – this will avoid a clash of expectations and possibly difficult parent meetings. Just as I am suggesting we need to share with children what the learning goals are for the activity, so we need to share our learning goals with parents. We are all learners, and what is good for one set of learners is good for another.

- Assessment should lead to better learning experiences, not just tick lists.
- The alternative model of assessment offers meaningful learning experiences.
- Learning is 'messy'; a linear approach to learning should be avoided.
- There is no one end point to learning; learning is an assortment of end points.
- Process should be more important than product.
- Parents need to understand the 'alternative model' of assessment.

Building up a picture

If we adopt this so-called alternative model of assessment then it is vital that we build up a picture of the child that comprises as much information as possible. Our 'one checklist or tick list', while useful, will only supply some information; it won't tell us all we need to know about the child.

It would seem that gathering data from a variety of sources would allow us to build up a holistic picture of the child which might be helpful. This data would come from the following sources:

- observation in the early years setting

- the children themselves

- parents

- peers.

Let's build up a picture of a young gifted and talented learner, called Anna, as we go along. We can then use this example to see how we can take forward Anna's learning.

Observation in the early years setting

Not all adults working with young children will be involved in formal observation of the children. However, all will be observing and making judgements on a daily basis. Indeed, educators often complain of spending so much time observing that they have no time to work with the children. However, structured, purposeful observation is a vital tool for the educator. Through observation we can not only monitor young children and their learning, but we can monitor our own actions and reactions to situations.

If we are going to observe then we have to be clear about what we are looking for. But herein lies a difficulty. Often we have in mind very clear aims for each activity and often these are shaped by national documentation. If we have very precise goals and learning outcomes then that is what we'll focus on and there is a real danger that we will miss the vital learning that is taking place because we are so focused on particular outcomes.

A 'tracking of achievement' sheet would allow us to gather information that will be useful for our final 'big picture'. Over time these sheets can be completed during a variety of activities, allowing a profile to be built up of individual children. They could be kept in a central file allowing open access and can be added to by anyone who sees something significant. Areas to be commented on would include:

- questioning

- understanding

- creativity

- logical thinking

- remembering

- working with others

- taking risks.

While these areas are not an exhaustive list, they are a starting point for the observation of gifted and talented learners. An example of such a sheet is given in Table 2.2, and there is a blank template that you can photocopy.

Table 2.2   Example observation sheet

TRACKING ACHIEVEMENT

Name of child: Anna

Category	Observation
Questioning	• Asks questions
	• Goes into details when answering questions
Understanding	• Demonstrates strong opinions/feelings
	• Extracts inferences
Creativity	• Inventor
	• Creates a new design
	• Is extremely inquisitive
	• Has 'madcap', impractical ideas
Logical thinking	• Thrives on complex activities
Remembering	• Is keenly observant
	• Manipulates information
Working with others	• Prefers to talk with adults
Takes risks	• Good at guessing but has to be encouraged to do so
Additional information	• Anna likes to get things right and isn't happy when made to have a go at something or when she thinks there's a chance she will 'get it wrong'.

Table 2.2a Observation sheet

OBSERVATION	
TRACKING ACHIEVEMENT	
Name of child:	
Category	**Observation**
Questioning	
Understanding	
Creativity	
Logical thinking	
Remembering	
Working with others	
Takes risks	
Additional information	

The child

Young gifted and talented children will know they can do certain things. Their families are often amazed at some of the things they can do and often the children themselves notice that they are good at things and can do things their friends can't. Often they know they can do things that their key workers and teachers don't know they can do. Sometimes that's because they don't get a chance to show these individuals what they can do. Let's think about this from Anna's perspective.

The library corner

Anna always gets excited when her key worker asks her to go to the library corner. She loves all kinds of books and likes nothing better than sitting on the big chair and reading a story. The only problem is that the key worker always reads the story to her. She loves having someone read a story to her, especially at bedtime, but she also likes reading a story for herself. She never really gets a chance to do that in the early years setting. They always sit in their groups and listen to the key worker and answer questions that the key worker asks. Her key worker knows she knows about words and books because she can answer all the questions he asks, but sometimes Anna has questions about the book too but she doesn't often get the chance to ask her questions. It's good that the children know about authors and illustrators and rhyming words and which way to turn the pages, but Anna wants to know why the author wrote the story that way or why the illustrator chose that colour or why the story ended the way it did – she never gets a chance to ask these kind of questions.

Anna has highlighted a number of issues for us, particularly related to reading:

- Young children are not always offered an opportunity to 'read' books for themselves.

- Discussions are often adult-led.

- Children have questions but are not always offered opportunities to ask these questions.

- In an effort to ensure that we cover the basic knowledge required for literacy activities, we tend to focus on certain aspects of literacy, which again are adult-led.

While not all children will be ready to participate at the level suggested by Anna, those who are, are being denied the opportunity to do so. While Anna has highlighted issues related to literacy and reading in particular, the same issues apply to all curricular areas.

One of the problems is that key workers ask questions about activities children do in the early years setting. So they say things like:

- How many ducks can you see in the picture?

- What are you going to put in that bit?

- How can you make your model move?

- Did you make that by yourself?

There's nothing wrong with these questions, but some children have lots of thoughts in their heads about things they can do or questions they want to ask and they don't often get a chance to talk to adults about them.

Children may tell us they like listening to music. Of course they will listen to music in the early years setting, but as the educator we may not know that children like listening to music at home. Armed with this knowledge, the educator can take time to talk to the children about music and to find out what kind of music they like to listen to.

Because life in the early years setting is busy and activities are often tightly organised and timetabled, we frequently miss opportunities to find out about the children and their interests and abilities. Sometimes this is because we don't ask questions about the wider world of the children. We focus on early years events and activities and often these are linked to assessment and attainment and the predetermined sets of knowledge and skills discussed earlier.

- Activities should not always be driven by the adult.
- Allow time for children to ask their own questions.
- Focus on wider aspects of learning such as attitude and motivation.

I asked some young gifted and talented learners what they were good at and what they enjoyed. It was interesting to discover that some children enjoyed things they did not perceive themselves to be particularly good at, while others were good at things they did not necessarily enjoy. This idea of the enjoyment of a task is interesting. When we enjoy something we are much more likely to participate. This disparity between enjoyment and competence could possibly lead to the label 'underachiever' being given when perhaps the child simply did not 'enjoy' the activity. This is worth being aware of and watching out for. Asking questions will help you in this.

Table 2.3 gives a sample of the kind of answers you might record when talking with a child. There is also a blank version for you to photocopy.

These questions offer a starting point for engaging young children in conversation and recording their answers. You will be able to think of many more questions but these should get you started. You should note that all children can be asked these questions and not just those that you 'think' might be gifted and talented.

Table 2.3   Children's interests and abilities

Name _____ *Anna* _____

1. What kind of things do you enjoy doing?

numbers		music	*yes*	exploring	
words	*yes*	art	*yes*	experimenting	
reading	*yes*	talking	*yes*	other	*yes*
sports		listening	*yes*		

If you said 'other' or something else, can you tell me a bit more about what it is you like doing?

Acting out stories. I like to be the characters in the story. My favourite is when I can be a princess. I like dressing up and dancing too.

2. What do you feel you are really good at?

numbers		music		exploring	
words	*yes*	art		experimenting	
reading	*yes*	talking	*yes*	other	*yes*
sports		listening			

If you said 'other' or something else, can you tell me a bit more about what it is you are really good at?

I'm really good at speaking out loud, like when we have to introduce something at the concert.

3. Have we helped you to become better at what you are good at?

Yes   *yes*   No   ☐

4. If yes, how have we helped you?

I got to introduce the song at the Christmas concert.

5. How do you know you're really good at doing something?

My mum and/or dad told me	*yes*	My friends told me	
A relative told me		I worked it out for myself	*yes*
My key worker told me	*yes*	Some other way	

6. Do you think there are others here who are good at the same things as you?

Yes   ☐   No   *no*

7. Would you like to work with someone who was good at the same things as you?

Yes   *yes*   No   ☐

Table 2.3a Children's interests and abilities

Name _____

1. What kind of things do you enjoy doing?

numbers		music		exploring	
words		art		experimenting	
reading		talking		other	
sports		listening			

If you said 'other' or something else, can you tell me a bit more about what it is you like doing?

2. What do you feel you are really good at?

numbers		music		exploring	
words		art		experimenting	
reading		talking		other	
sports		listening			

If you said 'other' or something else, can you tell me a bit more about what it is you are really good at?

3. Have we helped you to become better at what you are good at?

Yes ☐   No ☐

4. If yes, how have we helped you?

5. How do you know you're really good at doing something?

My mum and/or dad told me		My friends told me	
A relative told me		I worked it out for myself	
People at my nursery told me		Some other way	

6. Do you think there are others here who are good at the same things as you?

Yes ☐   No ☐

7. Would you like to work with someone who was good at the same things as you?

Yes ☐   No ☐

Gathering this kind of information allows you to begin to build up a picture of the child from the child's perspective. Engaging with children in conversation about their likes and dislikes and their abilities can make them feel a valued and important member of the early years setting. Remember that in Chapter 1 I argued that children use feedback from significant others to build up a personal theory relating to intelligence. You are a 'significant other' in the young child's life and showing this interest in them and their abilities will mean a lot to them.

- Take time just to 'talk' to the children.

- Know about the children's lives outside of the early years setting.

- Value the contributions each child can make to life in the early years setting.

- Use the information you have about children to plan their learning experiences.

Parents

Parents are often the source of valuable information for early years settings. They know the child better than anyone and see the child in different circumstances. They have much to contribute to the overall picture of a child and their abilities. However, often parents are viewed with suspicion. 'Every parent in my establishment would think their child is gifted' is a view sometimes expressed by educators. While undoubtedly difficulties arise when parents have unrealistically high expectations for their children, to ignore their opinions is equally dangerous. Often parents are reluctant to tell educators about their child's ability, as they fear they will be perceived as 'pushy' or 'prejudiced'. I asked some parents of older gifted and talented children to name one thing that they would have liked educators to do when their child was young. All the parents answered 'I wish they had believed me when I said my child had abilities'. Early years settings need to ensure that they create an ethos that allows parents to share information.

Such an ethos could be created by:

- being welcoming and friendly

- actively listening to parents

- sharing information with parents

- believing what parents tell you

- wanting to work in authentic partnership with parents.

If a parent indicates that they think their child might have particular abilities, it can be useful to find out a little more about these abilities. One way to do this would be to ask parents to complete a short questionnaire. Alternatively the questionnaire could be used as the basis for discussion and interview. The following sample questionnaire illustrates the kind of information you might record. Again, we also provide a photocopiable template. The questionnaire itself offers initial questions that will provide some information and act as a starter for discussion.

Table 2.4 Information from parents

Name of child Anna

1. At what age did you begin to think that your child had particular abilities? Please put an X in the appropriate box.

0–12months	☐	12–18 months	☐
18 months–24 months	[x]	2–3 years	☐
3–5 years	☐	5+ years	☐

2. Were you the first to notice your child's abilities?

Yes ☐   No [*no*]

If no, please state who first noticed and what they noticed

> *The health visitor. She was surprised Anna was asking about letters and knew sounds of letters at such an early age.*

3. In what area/s do your child's abilities lie?

music	*yes*	reading	*yes*
mathematics	*yes*	talking	*yes*
art		physical, e.g. sports, dance	
language	*yes*	good with people	*yes*
languages		science	
drama	*yes*	other/s	

If other/s, please state which _____

Further details/information about my child's abilities

> *Anna seems to have a very lively imagination. She is always dressing up and pretending to be a character from the book she is reading. She likes to talk with adults but then she spends a lot of time around adults. Her granny looks after her when I'm at work and she doesn't really have any younger cousins or relatives. She has started going to dancing and the teacher says she has very good rhythm and remembers the steps from one week to the next. She's always got her nose in a book. She also likes to watch television by turning down the sound and reading the subtitles.*

4. As a parent, how do you encourage, challenge and stretch your child's abilities at home?

Attend club/organisation	[*yes*]
Buy resources to support my child	[*yes*]
Use the computer/internet	☐
Talk to my child	[*yes*]
Take my child on outings/visits that relate to her ability	[*yes*]

Other

> *I like to try to make sure that Anna gets lots of opportunities to try things and not just things she's good at. However, we do go to the library three times a week.*

5. What could we do to work together with you to challenge and encourage your child?

> *I'm quite happy with what you are doing at the moment although I do worry a bit about what will happen when she goes to school. I don't want her to be bored.*

Thank you for completing this questionnaire.

Table 2.4a Information from parents

Name of child_____

1. At what age did you begin to think that your child had particular abilities? Please put an X in the appropriate box.

   0–12months ☐   12–18 months ☐
   18 months–24 months ☐   2–3 years ☐
   3–5 years ☐   5+ years ☐

2. Were you the first to notice your child's abilities?

   Yes ☐   No ☐

   If no, please state who first noticed and what they noticed

3. In what area/s do your child's abilities lie?

music		reading	
mathematics		talking	
art		physical, e.g. sports, dance	
language		good with people	
languages		science	
drama		other/s	

   If other/s, please state which _____

   Further details/information about my child's abilities

4. As a parent, how do you encourage, challenge and stretch your child's abilities at home?

   Attend club/organisation ☐
   Buy resources to support my child ☐
   Use the computer/internet ☐
   Talk to my child ☐
   Take my child on outings/visits that relate to her ability ☐

   Other

5. What could we do to work together with you to challenge and encourage your child?

Thank you for completing this questionnaire.

Peers

Gardner (1983) would argue that being good with other people and knowing about yourself are intelligences that need to be recognised, nurtured and developed. Anyone working with young children will know that mostly they are interested in 'themselves' first and foremost. This 'egocentric' approach to life is part of growing up and development. I have witnessed young children making very hurtful comments to one another – 'you're really stupid', 'you're being silly'. If young children can make these kinds of judgement about their peers, then they may well be capable of making more positive judgements about their peers too. To see if children had the ability to think beyond themselves, I tried asking young children who would be good at helping me with certain activities in the early years setting? Answers to these types of questions allow us to see how young children view their peers and give us an insight into their stage of interaction. The answers to my questions broadly fell into three categories:

1   Me – I would be good at helping you.

2   Me and my friend would be good at helping you.

3   My friend or others in the nursery would be good at helping you.

The first category of answer was most common among the children.

For example:

Staff:	*Who would be a good person to help me with jigsaws?*
Child:	*Me*
Staff:	*Who would be a good person to help me cut out shapes?*
Child:	*Me*

Reasons for this may include:

• they were not ready to 'see beyond themselves'

• they are trying to establish 'goodness and badness' and they wanted me to know how good they were (this links to the work of Carol Dweck, which was outlined in Chapter 1).

The second category of answer suggests some awareness of others and their abilities in the early years setting, and often the other names included those in their friendship group. For example:

Staff:	*Who would be a good person to help me with jigsaws?*
Child:	*Me and my friend*
Staff:	*Who would be a good person to help me cut out shapes?*
Child:	*Me and my two friends*

Children who were 'very able' most commonly gave the third category of answer in a range of areas, e.g. motor control, language, number, art, etc. They were also all very articulate. They demonstrated a level of understanding about their peers and themselves not seen in the other children. They also offered an explanation for their choice of name, almost as though they were providing evidence for their choice. For example:

Staff:	*Who would be a good person to help me with jigsaws?*
Child:	*Frida, she's very good at jigsaws and I'm quite good too*
Staff:	*Who would be a good person to help me cut out shapes?*
Child:	*Stuart, he cuts very carefully*

In answer to this last question, one child also replied 'that would have to be me, I'm definitely the best at cutting out in this nursery!' While the child being questioned still featured in the answers, there did not appear to be the same need to be 'first' and they also demonstrated an ability to reflect and think about the answer before giving a name. While the friends of the children I interviewed featured in their answers, they included other children in the early years setting and appeared more aware of the larger group.

Asking questions will give you the opportunity to gauge where children are in their development. It will also allow you to begin to build up a social picture of the early years setting. You will see friendship groups emerging. Don't be surprised when undertaking this activity if you discover that not all the children know each other's names. It never ceases to amaze me how often we take this for granted, and yet closer inspection often reveals that a child can tell you what another child is good at but not their name – 'him, the boy with the red jumper, he's good at football!'

The following pages offer a framework for questioning. The questions have tried to take into account a range of curricular areas and skills including:

- fine motor skills

- motor development

- musical ability

- emotional intelligence

- mathematical ability

- literacy

- communication and language.

You will be able to add to this list and adapt it so that it fits the requirements of your early years setting. A sample shows you the kind of answers you might be given as you discuss this with the children. There is a blank template for you to photocopy.

Who is good at what? Some questions to get you started

Sit with the child in a quieter area of the early years setting. Use the following script to help you frame the scene.

Adult: I've got lots of jobs that need to be done and I want to try to find girls and boys who could help me do these jobs. I'm going to tell you what I need done and then ask you who you think would be a good person to do this job. Perhaps you think more than one person might be good at this job. If you do, that's OK.

Table 2.5   Who is good at what? Some questions to get you started

Name of child: Anna	
Question	**Nomination**
If I couldn't finish a jigsaw, who would I ask to help me?	*Jemma and Hope*
Who would I ask to help me cut out shapes?	*Jack*
Who would I choose to be in my sports team?	*Kwaku*
Who should I choose to sing my favourite song?	*Rachael*
If I fell and hurt myself, who would be good to take care of me?	*Jack and me*
If I had to do some counting and needed help, whom would I ask?	*Robin*
Who should I choose to paint my picture?	*Me*
If I had to choose someone to read a book with me, whom should I choose?	*Me*
If I had to pick someone to speak to the boys and girls, whom should I choose?	*Me*
If I had to choose someone to play an instrument, whom should I choose?	*Hope and me*
If I needed someone to solve a puzzle, whom should I choose?	*Robin*
If I needed someone to talk to, who would be a good friend?	*Jordan and me*

- Include the child in the data-gathering process.

- Value the views of parents. Offer parents an opportunity to share their views.

- Involve all the children in the identification process.

- Be interested in how the children learn, not just what they produce.

Table 2.5a Who is good at what? Some questions to get you started

Sit with the child in a quieter area of the early years setting. Use the following script to help you frame the scene.

Adult: I've got lots of jobs that need to be done and I want to try to find girls and boys who could help me do these jobs. I'm going to tell you what I need done and then ask you who you think would be a good person to do this job. Perhaps you think more than one person might be good at this job. If you do, that's OK.

Name of child:

Question	Nomination
If I couldn't finish a jigsaw, who would I ask to help me?	
Who would I ask to help me cut out shapes?	
Who would I choose to be in my sports team?	
Who should I choose to sing my favourite song?	
If I fell and hurt myself, who would be good to take care of me?	
If I had to do some counting and needed help, whom would I ask?	
Who should I choose to paint my picture?	
If I had to choose someone to read a book with me, whom should I choose?	
If I had to pick someone to speak to the boys and girls, whom should I choose?	
If I had to choose someone to play an instrument, whom should I choose?	
If I needed someone to solve a puzzle, whom should I choose?	
If I needed someone to talk to, who would be a good friend?	

Pulling it all together

You have gathered data from four sources:

- observation

- the child

- the parent

- peers.

It's important to look at it all and to decide what it is telling you. One way to do this is to identify four key things from each source that you think are important and note them on a 'Big Picture' sheet. Having noted them on this summary sheet, you will begin to get an overall picture of the child and their abilities. From this you can start to decide how you can challenge the child to develop these abilities further through the activities easily made available in the early years setting.

Having taken Anna as an example, we know some things about her already but if we put our knowledge together, what does the big picture suggest we need to be doing? The following sample sheet shows us what we already know. A blank photocopiable template follows.

This overview can then be used to plan learning experiences for children as national policy and curriculam frameworks are implemented in the setting.

Cultural differences and international approaches

One of the ways that culture impacts on education is through the policies and approaches a country adopts. Our education systems are rooted in our culture and

Table 2.6   The big picture

Name of child: Anna
Name/s of staff: Mina

Observation	Key points
	1. manipulates information
	2. thrives on complex activities
	3. goes into detail, expands
	4. initiates tasks
Parents	Key points
	1. been asking about sounds and letters from an early age
	2. reads all the time
	3. turns down the sound on TV and reads the subtitles
	4. often visits the library

(Continued)

Table 2.6   (Continued)

Child	Key points
	1. enjoys language-related activities
	2. is really good at reading
	3. would like to work with others
	4. has a good self-awareness
Peers	**Key points**
	1. has a wide range of friends
	2. can appreciate others' abilities
	3. can identify abilities in others
	4. strong interpersonal skills

history. Internationally there have been early years curricula developments that have sought to meet the needs of all young children. Some of these such as Te Whāriki (MoE, 1995), Reggio Emilia (Malaguzzi, 1996), Head Start and High Scope Programme (USA) and the Sure Start and The Foundation Stage (UK) are examples of developments which have become widely used or have influenced early years care and education outside of their country of origin. While these frameworks do not explicitly discuss gifted and talented children, they do offer opportunities for educators to develop activities and think about planning learning for high ability. Curricula in many parts of the world, and certainly in the UK, are undergoing significant change. Rather than focusing on particular documentation we will look at the influence of culture on what we do and consider some of the generic issues facing countries across the globe as they seek to cater for children who are gifted and talented.

An educational theorist called Jerome Bruner argues that culture shapes the mind and is shaped by the mind, and that this gives us the mechanism by which we can make sense of the world and our place within it. He talks about the 'culture of childhood' (Bruner, 1996). Any thinking in which we engage is therefore rooted in our culture.

The *Collins Concise English Dictionary* defines culture as

> the total of the inherited ideas, beliefs, values and knowledge, which constitute the shared basis of social action. (Collins, 1988)

The communities that you and your children come from will have definite cultures. Often communities can be melting pots of cultural experiences and exchanges but it is likely that out of this will come a dominant culture and it is this which will influence you, the children and their families. We are all products of our different cultures. This will impact on your thinking and understanding of learning.

As well as a national and local or community culture, there will be an early years setting culture. This is influenced and shaped by management. There will be a culture within your room that has been created and shaped by your experiences and the experiences of those in the room. It may change from year to year as you work with different year groups. It will undoubtedly influence how you approach tasks and interact with the children and how they interact with each other.

Table 2.6a The big picture

Name of child:

Name/s of staff:

Observation	Key points
	1.
	2.
	3.
	4.
Parents	Key points
	1.
	2.
	3.
	4.
Child	Key points
	1.
	2.
	3.
	4.
Peers	Key points
	1.
	2.
	3.
	4.

 Photocopiable:
Gifted and Talented in the Early Years (2nd edition) © Margaret Sutherland, 2012 (SAGE)

If we want to support young children in their learning, we need to have an understanding of the significant influences on their lives. What they believe and are influenced by may well affect how they approach life in an early years setting. What you believe and are influenced by will affect your expectations and how you approach the early years setting. Arriving at some shared understanding of this may help us to support the children's learning.

Some children will come from homes where learning and education are revered; others will come from homes where education is secondary to dealing with life issues.

Your ideas about learning and ability will be based on:

- your own experiences

- the culture from which you come

- the culture in which you work.

- We need to be aware of the dominant culture.

- We need to be aware of the impact culture has on learning.

- We need to consider what kind of culture we have developed in our early years setting.

Internationally, giftedness is of great interest to educators and politicians alike. How can we ensure that we develop the talents and abilities of upcoming generations in a way that might address big issues of global concern such as poverty, food security and climate change in the future? Each country develops provision according to its history, culture and existing education system. But regardless of differences between countries there would appear to be some commonalities in relation to gifted education. Different countries are generally concerned about:

- ensuring provision is not elitist, particularly in times of austerity

- developing and providing quality training for educators

- developing identification processes that encompasses more than IQ

- valuing and providing for academic ability as much as sport, music, dance, art, etc.

These concerns can be seen in the way various countries conceptualise gifted education and develop provision. Common responses to the conundrum of how to best educate gifted children include pull-out programmes, talent centres, talent searches, grade skipping, specialised gifted training progammes for educators, personalisation of the curriculum and flexibility of the age of entry to school, to name but a few. Much of the writing relating to these approaches is concerned with school-age children and young adults and often it is based in the USA. It is interesting to note that international studies that specifically examine giftedness in young children are conspicuous by their absence. However, I would argue that bringing together current developments and initiatives in early years education with current studies in giftedness may offer us an opportunity to develop culturally appropriate learning opportunities for young children that go some way to developing practice in the new paradigm we discussed in Chapter 1.

The international debate around the nature of intelligence and the best place to educate gifted children will no doubt continue in the future. In the early years settings we have a unique opportunity to start children on their learning journey. Whatever our country, culture and history we need to provide challenge through the curriculam and engage children in the learning process.

Summing up

Some key points about the identification of gifted and talented learners have been made in this chapter.

- Labels for children are not always necessary, but challenging learning experiences are.
- Assessment should be about learning, not plugging gaps in knowledge and skills.
- We need to build up the whole picture of the child's abilities and interests.
- The information we gather can help us to plan next steps and challenging learning experiences.
- Culture plays a part in the learning process.
- There are common issues relating to gifted education being discussed internationally.

Useful websites

www.mensa.org.uk This website contains interesting information including a handy checklist of behaviour characteristics and things to look out for in your setting.

www.teachingexpertise.com/topic/curriculum-development This website considers aspects of curriculum change.

Further reading

Balchin, T., Hymer, B. and Matthews, D. (2009) (eds) *The Routledge International Companion to Gifted Education.* Abingdon: Routledge.

Carr, M. (2001) *Assessment in Early Childhood Settings.* London: SAGE Publications.

3

Activities and resources

This chapter will consider:

> - **The cross-curricular nature of problem-solving.**
> - **The importance of developing thinking skills across the curriculum.**
> - **The common resources and activities on offer across four specific curricular areas.**
> - **The skills and abilities gifted and talented children might present in each of these curricular areas.**

So far we have looked at how to gather information about children's abilities from four main sources:

- observation in the early years setting

- the children themselves

- parents

- peers.

To focus our attention on aspects of learning we will now think about particular curricular areas and what young children might be doing during various activities. We will consider four curricular areas:

- physical movement/motor development

- music

- language

- mathematics.

While this chapter suggests advanced responses that young children might demonstrate, I am in no way suggesting that they can automatically be labelled 'gifted and talented' just because they can demonstrate these abilities. What I am suggesting is that if this is what they can do already, then we need to be aware of this and decide how we will challenge them next time they arrive at the gym, the music corner or wherever. They can't just do more of the same.

Before we look at individual curricular areas we will think about thinking. As the role of IQ in the identification process of gifted and talented has been questioned, there has been an increased interest in thinking skills and how we can develop them, as it is recognised that advanced thinking skills may be relevant to the identification process. While thinking is inextricably linked to other aspects of learning and skills, e.g. talking, we will consider thinking at this juncture as it is an integral part of early years practice.

Thinking

Thinking seems to underpin learning and so the argument goes if we improve our capacity to think, we will improve our capacity to learn. Many people have written about thinking skills and their importance in the learning and teaching process. People such as Bloom (1956), Ennis (1962), de Bono (1976), Fisher (1990), Lipman (1991), Gilhooly (1996) and Wallace (2002) all point to the need to develop thinking skills.

Within early years two approaches towards thinking skills can often be seen. McGuiness (1999) calls them infusion approaches and discrete approaches. Within an infusion model opportunities for thinking are built into the curriculum. Discrete approaches involve the use of techniques and particular programmes or resources to encourage thinking. Within early years settings the infusion approach can commonly be seen, with practitioners picking up on a child's interests and developing activities and opportunities for thinking from this (Siraj-Blatchford and Sylva, 2004). Philosophy for Children (P4C), Thinking Actively in a Social Context (TASC) (Wallace, 2002) and Thinking Together (Mercer, 2000) are examples of discrete approaches that can often be seen in early years settings.

Cognitive thinking refers to the mental processes we use. The kinds of activities we engage in when we think include:

- asking questions

- solving problems

- making decisions

- recalling information

- interpreting

- visualising

- hypothesising.

Thinking about thinking is known as metacognition – in other words, thinking about how we make use of the cognitive skills listed above. Developing 'metacognition' or 'knowing about knowing' alongside thinking skills will result in children knowing when and how to use particular strategies for learning or problem solving.

A report by Walsh, Murphy and Dunbar (2007) looked at literature and case studies about thinking and thinking skills in order to offer some practical guidance to practitioners. The report suggests there are six things settings need to take account of if they are going to support children's thinking:

- **Social/emotional development**

   Are children adequately confident to tackle ambiguity and express their point of view?

- **Motivation and dispositions to learn**

   Do children show adequate persistence to stay with a problem and to think it through?

- **Cognitive development**

   Have children developed the capacity to sequence and order, classify and sort at a concrete level?

- **Linguistic development**

   Have children acquired the linguistic competence to explain and give reasons?

   Can they explain why they have done things in a certain way, discuss their plan of action and answer open-ended questions?

- **Creative development**

   Do children show a degree of imagination and flair in what they do?

- **Reflective responses**

   Can children ask questions and express the need to find out more?

   Can children be to some extent, self-critical, accept suggestions from others, tackle ambiguity and be open to challenge?

(Walsh et.al., 2007: 3–4)

If we think about thinking skills like this we will see that they are an intrinsic part of good learning and teaching for all. In order to be able to think, children must have some background knowledge about the topic under consideration. Gifted and talented children will often have a considerable amount of knowledge about a topic but sometimes they are not always sure what to do with this knowledge. Their peers are not interested as the subject area is one that has no appeal for them. Sometimes the gifted child might know more about a subject than the adults around them. The role of the practitioner is crucial in this situation. Practitioners need to support children to become proficient in their thinking. If we do this we will be offering them skills that they will use long after they have graduated from the education system.

The table below outlines possible issues that may arise if we don't take account of the kind of thinking that some gifted and talented children engage in.

Characteristics	Potential issues
Retain a significant number of facts	Can become bored in the setting
Excellent long-term memory	Can become bored in the setting
A 'quick' thinker	May become frustrated when working with others who think more slowly
A creative thinker	Adults and peers may see them as troublesome
Has original ideas	Not keen to conform
Wacky or out of the ordinary solutions	Others may view them as being slightly 'odd'. They may feel misunderstood by those around them
Apparently hare-brained ideas	Others may view them as being slightly 'odd'. They may feel misunderstood by those around them and find it difficult to work collaboratively on a task
A deep thinker	Keeps asking questions and probing for answers. May not be satisfied with an initial answer
Can think in abstract terms	May be concerned with the 'big issues' in life such as life and death

Using discerete approaches such as the ones mentioned earlier can be helpful to children and practitioners alike as they allow children to work and learn at their own pace and depth, but also allow them to contribute to their peer group learning. When this happens the learning for all becomes richer.

When planning thinking experiences and activities for gifted and talented young children practitioners need to consider:

- discovering what existing knowledge about the topic the child has

- developing activities that take account of that knowledge and allow the child to deepen their knowledge further

- ensuring children have times to work with intellectual peers

- valuing the information and expertise the children have by allowing them to contribute to the group learning

- asking open-ended, probing questions of children as they participate in the activity

- accepting all ideas and encouraging children to explore them and helping them to test them out

- never dismissing an area of concern or interest a child may have.

The diagram below demonstrates how learning should delve deeper into a topic but should also continue on an upwards trajectory. This 'delving down to reach up' model allows us to see how learning moves the learner forward but also highlights how it is a continuous process. Carefully crafted questions that allow thinking to develop can help build this model.

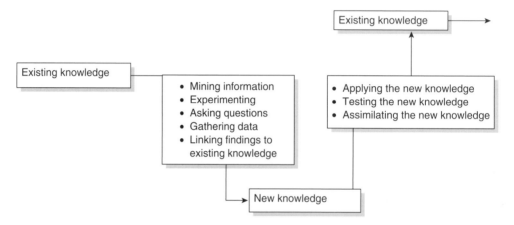

Figure 3.1 Delving down to reach up

One issue that can raise its head in the setting is when a young gifted and talented child's ability to think is sometimes well in advance of their ability to record their thoughts. Practitioners need to consider ways that young children can record their thoughts in an appropriate format other than the traditional methods of formal writing. These might include:

- pictures using a variety of media

- composing a piece of music

- sculpture

- recording on CD

- movie making

- digital photography

- having someone scribe

- explanation through drama, e.g. use of puppets, story-telling, plays.

This is not an exhaustive list but gives the practitioner a starting point. It should be noted that many of these formats allow for the development of skills beyond subject areas and knowledge content.

Helping children to think and to articulate their thoughts are important aspects of the practitioner's work.

Planning

One of the first things to do, regardless of what skill you want to challenge, is to plan the activity. Planning an activity allows you to think about where the children are in their learning and how you would like to move their learning forward. It also offers you an opportunity to talk with the children and find out what they're interested in and how they like to learn. For example, some children will be:

- *active* learners – they like to learn by doing

- *visual* learners – they like to learn by watching

- *participative* learners – they like to learn by copying a more knowledgeable other.

Knowing about how the child likes to learn will help you to plan more appropriate learning tasks.

While the focus here is on young children who are already displaying some degree of ability, this outline can be used for planning the learning of any child. Planning requires the following to be considered:

- What can the child already do?

- Is the child working independently on the skill?

- Are the present activities too easy for the child?

- What is the child interested in?

- Where do I want to take their learning next?

- What is the best way to help them get there?

- Implications for organisation.

A planning framework sheet where you can jot down some answers to these questions will allow you to think about how you will challenge a child's learning. You can also add these to the child's folio. Over time this will result in a developmental picture of the planning that has taken place for that child.

Table 3.1 What can children do and what next?

Question	Comment
What can the child already do?	
Is the child working independently?	
In what ways are the present activities too easy for the child?	
What do I want the child to learn? Relate to learning Outcomes/desirable Outcomes	
What is the best way to help them to learn?	
Implications for organisation	

Planning framework

With the planning framework in mind, the rest of this chapter suggests activities that will allow you to challenge young children and take forward their learning. They have been developed with the busy educator in mind. They offer ready-to-use activities that can be adapted to suit the needs of individual early years settings.

Photocopy these pages and keep them in a ring binder. You can add to them as you develop activities yourself. If you keep them in a central place, everyone can access them. This will allow your early years setting to build up a bank of challenging activities.

> Competence in the activities and skills listed in this chapter are examples only and do not necessarily mean a child should be labelled gifted and talented. It does mean that they need to be challenged.

Physical movement/motor development

Why physical movement and motor development?

- Children from all countries and cultures engage in physical activity.

- Children enjoy physical activities and many would rather engage in this than other kinds of tasks.

- Children's health and general well-being can be enhanced through physical activities.

- Children's development in these areas can positively influence other forms of learning.

It has been suggested in the media that, in the UK, we are not doing enough to develop the talents and abilities of young athletes. Much discussion about this issue took place during the 2004 Olympic Games in Athens and in the run up to the 2012 Olympic Games in London. Notwithstanding the debate about how young you start coaching children, neglecting physical movement and motor development and children who show particular ability in this area is likely to impact not only on a country's medal-winning chances at future Olympic Games, but also on the development of children generally – physically, emotionally and academically. Coupled with the growing concern over childhood obesity, can we really afford to neglect this vital aspect of the curriculum?

Young children love to move. Indeed, they spend much of their time moving, and yet this important aspect of their development is all too easily overlooked as we focus on the important areas of numeracy and literacy skills. The significance of motor development in relation to learning generally should not be underestimated. Competence in physical movement and motor development will greatly enhance learning across the curriculum, including those important areas of numeracy and literacy.

Motor development in the early years is primarily concerned with:

- improving coordination

- control

- manipulation

- movement.

There are some key skills in all of this that the educator will be looking for when working with children.

A starting point for consideration is how well developed the children's fine and gross motor skills are. In other words, how well do they make small and big movements? Competence in these areas will offer a strong starting place for future work in a range of curricular areas. Children who are gifted and talented in physical activities may well present highly developed skills and abilities relating to physical movement and motor development.

So what will these children be able to do? Generally, when looking for competence in **fine motor skills**, children will be able to easily complete the following tasks:

- fasten and unfasten buttons on their clothes/buckles on their shoes

- cut out shapes using scissors

- colour within lines

- rotate their palms upwards/downwards

- attempt to tie their shoe laces

- use a knife and fork when eating

- touch each finger with their thumb (right and left hands)

- build a tower of bricks.

It can be seen how several of these skills, for example colouring within lines, will be detected in other curricular areas. However, the trick for the educator is to use these skills in a cross-curricular manner and to see the relationship between colouring in and physical movement and motor development and then to challenge children in all areas.

Generally, when looking for competence in **gross motor skills**, children will be able to easily complete the following tasks:

- hop just as well on both legs

- gallop with the left or the right foot in front

- balance on one leg without wobbling about for five seconds

- using a heel-to-toe action, walk along a straight line

- bounce a large ball with one hand

- catch a large ball each time with both hands

- jump and land with both feet together

- stop and start quickly when travelling round a space

- curve, curl and stretch out the body

- run around in a large space without bumping into anyone or anything.

These skills underpin many aspects of physical movement and motor development. While there are many approaches to physical movement and motor development, we are going to concentrate on skills. The development of skills is important, not only for those who may be gifted and talented, but for all young children in our care.

Let's think about the activities we offer in our early years setting. We will consider what we might see children doing during certain activities and we will also consider what children already proficient in particular skills will be doing. We will look at five common activities and their related resources in an early years setting:

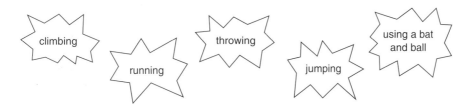

Climbing

Even before they can walk, young children are using climbing actions to pull themselves along the floor or onto furniture. Young children also have a fascination for stairs and will experiment by clambering up and down stairs with bottoms in the air and much effort being expended. Often when left to play, young children will climb up fences, walls and trees. This desire to climb often leaves parents and educators alike holding their breath. However, in an early years setting there are controlled opportunities to develop this natural ability and curiosity.

The climbing frame, whether outdoors or indoors, offers wonderful opportunities for gross motor development. With guidance and support, children can become confident climbers.

Resource: Climbing apparatus

Activity/resources	Responses	Advanced responses
Climbing, e.g. on apparatus	• be nervous when using the equipment and perhaps even be reluctant to join in • take great effort to hold body weight • be erratic and hesitant when climbing • use same arm/leg action • have a weak grasp of the bars	• have confidence on apparatus • hold body weight with ease • display effortless, flowing a movements as they climb • use opposite arm/leg action • have a strong grasp of the bars

Running

When faced with a large open space, young children zoom around, often shrieking and screaming with delight as the wind whips through their hair. The whole body is involved in running – arms to propel them forward, long steps to cover ground quickly. Running with purpose and control takes some degree of skill and young children can often be seen running so fast that they can't stop. It is the educators' job to support children and help them to experience the joy of running.

Resource: Large spaces

Activity/resources	Responses	Advanced responses
Running	• overstated lean • uncoordinated action • flailing leg and arm movement • head forward • not in the air much during the running process • lower leg 'flaps' about	• bent forwards • flowing action • leg and arm movements in opposition to each other • during the running process the runner is in the air • the supporting leg is firm and extended

Throwing and catching

From an early age children throw things. Frequently they may throw away something they don't want, e.g. their soft toy. At first the throw can be 'floppy' with little control over where the object lands or the distance it is thrown. Later the throw can be more deliberate and controlled – such as when a child is throwing something away in a temper, the object may be thrown at someone or something to reinforce a point and communicate how the child is feeling. There should of course be a more positive reason for throwing something, such as when we play with a ball. There are three main ways of throwing an object:

- underarm

- overarm

- sideways.

Each throw has a specific purpose; e.g. overarm would be the choice for throwing something a distance. The educator can work with young children to help them acquire greater accuracy in throwing and help them to select the right throw for the activity. There is also ample opportunity for the educator to discuss when you should throw something and the safety aspects involved in throwing objects. As children develop hand and eye coordination their ability to catch develops.

Resources: Large balls, beanbags, small balls, quoits

Activity/resources	Responses	Advanced responses
Throwing, e.g. overarm throw	<ul><li>very little backswing</li><li>poor transference of weight</li><li>non-throwing arm hangs limply at side</li><li>steps forward on same leg as throwing arm</li><li>child has difficulty releasing the object in the correct direction</li></ul>	<ul><li>arm swings back prior to throw</li><li>weight transfers forwards</li><li>non-throwing arm is held out to aid balance</li><li>steps forward on opposite foot to throwing arm</li><li>throwing arm follows through towards the direction of the throw</li></ul>
Catching	<ul><li>scoops the ball to their chest</li></ul>	<ul><li>uses forearms with elbows bent to catch a ball efficiently and securely</li></ul>

Jumping

Young children can often be seen jumping up and down with excitement. Jumping into the air from one foot or two feet and landing again on one foot or two feet requires some degree of control. In fact, often the landing is the tricky bit for young children and frequently a jump ends with a child wobbling and losing his/her balance. The educator can work with the child to overcome these difficulties thus ensuring, among other things, a safe landing.

Resource: Flat space

Using a bat and ball

This is perhaps one of the most difficult skills to perform. When using a bat and ball a number of skills come into play at one time. For example, hand–eye coordination is essential, especially when this involves using an object other than a part of the body. Being able to focus on a ball as it travels through the air and track it until it makes contact with the bat is also a highly developed skill.

For some children these skills will develop as they mature and progress through the education system. A structured programme can support children as they develop.

Resources: Various size balls, various size bats

Activity/resources	Responses	Advanced responses
Using a bat and ball	<ul><li>does not prepare to hit the ball</li><li>body faces the front</li><li>stance does not alter</li><li>eyes do not make contact with the ball</li><li>bat 'stabs' at ball</li></ul>	<ul><li>bat is in position to receive the ball</li><li>body faces the side in preparation</li><li>weight is moved to front foot</li><li>eyes follow the ball through the air</li><li>bat hits ball with sweeping action</li></ul>

Music

Why music?

- From birth, young children take part in vocal play.

- First musical experiences are known to shape future interest in music.

- Music allows children to express and develop their feelings and emotions.

- There are links between musical development and development in the other creative media, e.g. word/sound rhythms, syllables.

- Making music, both individually and collectively, is good fun.

- Music provides an ideal opportunity for listening for sound and word patterns in a fun way.

- Music develops memory skills.

Music is often an area in which educators lack confidence. They claim they 'can't sing a note' or are 'tone deaf'. Consequently, depending on the ability and confidence of staff in the early years setting, music may be paid scant attention. However, we know that music is important for aspects of human development. Music is all around us – on TV, on the radio, in supermarkets. Music is used to create atmosphere and is a powerful tool for communicating our emotions.

As educators we have a responsibility to nurture music-making. By doing this we will encourage children to build up their musical confidence and may well do the same for the adults involved.

Let's think about the activities we offer in our early years setting. We will consider what we might see children doing during certain activities and we will also consider what children who are already proficient, will be doing. We will look at some common activities and their related resources in an early years setting:

Singing

Singing is a natural expression for humans. Babies gurgle and babble and we know that they respond to songs with a strong beat. Young children appear to enjoy singing familiar songs over and over again. They experiment with their voices and often begin to gain confidence in singing aloud. While the repetition of songs is helpful, young children also relish the opportunity to learn new songs and this offers the early years educator the possibility of drawing on the wealth of materials around.

Resources: Nursery rhymes, action songs, counting songs, echo songs, tapes, CDs

Activity/resources	Responses	Advanced responses
Singing a song. 'Okki Tokki Unga': Action Songs for Children; Apusskidu: Songs for Children; Mango Spice: 44 Caribbean Songs; Tongo: Count Me In: 44 Songs and Rhymes about Numbers; Tom Thumb's Musical Maths: Developing Maths Skills with Simple Songs; etc.	• doesn't participate • shows no interest • easily distracted • poor memory for words • monotone • don't recognise familiar songs	• enthusiastic • responds to activities • can hold a tune • makes up songs • enjoys performing • recognises familiar songs in varying contexts, e.g. on TV

Instruments and sound-making

Babies begin to explore sound when, for example, they shake their rattle. They discover that different rattles produce different sounds. As they become older and progress to such things as banging pots and pans, they also begin to realise that not only do different pots produce different sounds but also that the sounds produced are not always welcomed by the adults around them. The adults often tightly control the playing of instruments and other sound-making equipment in the early years setting. This may inhibit creativity and exploration. Young children need time to develop this aspect of music making.

Resources: Tuned percussion instruments, e.g. chime bars, hand chimes, piano; untuned percussion, e.g. drums, woodblocks, bells, shakers, triangles, cymbals, tambourines

Activity/resources	Responses	Advanced responses
Instruments and sound-making	• has to be shown each time how to hold and play the instrument • plays the instrument erratically • plays the instrument at inappropriate times	• remembers how to hold and play the instrument • has control over their movements when playing • can play as part of a group at appropriate times • can pick out a tune on an instrument • can recognise different instruments
Keeping the beat using untuned percussion instruments	• erratic • lack of coordination • lack of muscle control • lack of awareness of others participating	• keeps regular beat • strong control of movements • can vary pace • can tap back simple rhythms • can make up simple rhythms
Dynamic, e.g. high/ low; fast/slow; loud/ soft	• cannot differentiate sounds • cannot select appropriate dynamic for a situation, e.g. quiet for sleeping	• can differentiate sounds • can select appropriate dynamic for a situation, e.g. loud for a storm

Music appreciation

Children hear music all the time but this should not be equated with listening to music. Listening to pre-recorded music has an important role to play in children's musical development. While it can never replace listening to 'live music', it can nevertheless be used to create an atmosphere where children are encouraged to respond to what they hear.

Resources: CDs, DVDs, sound tracks

Activity/resources	Responses	Advanced responses
Listening to a piece of music e.g. *Peter and the Wolf*, Debussy	• no facial response to the music • no body response to the music	• offers an emotional response • sways in time to the music • recognises the music, e.g. 'that sounds like...'

Activity/resources	Responses	Advanced responses
	• no awareness that music can communicate feelings • no recognition of having previously heard the music • not interested in listening to new pieces of music	• can equate a time/place/event with the music • can re-create the music, e.g. through singing later • asks to hear favourite pieces of music • asks to hear new pieces of music • can identify musical sounds from the environment

Literacy and Language

Why literacy and language?

• Language allows us to express feelings and thoughts.

• Language allows us to communicate with one another.

• Language allows us to think in the abstract.

Perhaps at the core of language is an ability to communicate – our thoughts, feelings and opinions. Human beings of course start to communicate from the minute they are born. Facial gestures and non-verbal communication lay the early building blocks for later communication through speech. A child's first words help us to see how the child is making sense of his/her world. Quickly he/she learns to combine words and begins to understand the power of language. Language also allows us to think in the abstract and to muse over complex ideas. Many parents of children who are gifted and talented in language report that their children began talking earlier than expected. These children may also show a keen interest in letters and written language sooner than their chronological age would suggest. Literacy education is seen to be key in empowering individuals personally and also in relation to encouraging and enabling them to become active members of society. It has been recognised that different literacies exist in different contexts and some children arrive in the setting fluent in the dominant literacy in the setting – they understand how it works and how to participate in activities. Language has traditionally been connected to the development of speech and reading and the conveying of meaning. If some children are fluent in the dominant literacy of the setting and are articulate and can read it is little wonder they are sometimes regarded as being gifted and talented.

Early years educators need to offer rich literacy and language opportunities for all children to ensure that they become the empowered individuals mentioned previously. This idea is picked up again in Chapter 6.

Let's think about the activities we offer in our early years setting. We will consider what we might see children doing during certain activities and we will also consider what children already proficient in particular skills will be doing. While it is acknowledged that there are different ways of being literate, we will look at four common activities and their related resources in an early years setting:

Talking

Children are born communicating and their experiences thus far will have shaped and determined how articulate they have become. Certainly many young children can talk a great deal, although not all of it is meaningful to the adult. There are many occasions in the early years setting that lend themselves to the development of this skill. It is the job of the early years educator to support and develop talk through everyday interaction with the children so that all can participate in this fundamental life skill.

Resources: Books, pictures, games, artwork, circle time, snack time

Activity/resources	Responses	Advanced responses
Retelling a story	• recounts the story out of sequence • repeats parts of the story • gives facts about the characters • unlikely to predict the outcome • factual talk	• recounts story sequentially • recounts the story with accurate details • 'reads between the lines' • predicts the outcome from the clues so far • uses adjectives • can create an atmosphere
Recounting an experience	• gets muddled up with sequence of events • becomes frustrated and starts to repeat themselves • concerned only with themselves	• recounts events precisely • uses expression to make a point • will talk about others as well as themselves
Communicating with peers	• no initiation of conversation • talks in parallel with peers • changes the topic	• initiates conversation • interacts and engages in the conversation • elaborates on the topic
Explaining something, e.g. their art work	• factual talk • repeats what they have heard others say • cannot give reason for personal response	• uses adjectives • gives reasons for their response • can give a personal reason for their response

Listening/watching

Listening and watching are skills that need to be practised and honed. Indeed, there are some adults who struggle to truly listen to what is being said or see what is happening around them. However, if we are to come to some kind of understanding with our fellow human beings then listening to what they have to say is vital. Similarly, watching, when you really absorb the details of things, takes time and practice too. Helping young children to develop these skills will pay dividends in the future.

Resources: Story tapes, books, songs

Activity/resources	Responses	Advanced responses
Listening to instructions	• does not focus on what is being said • cannot repeat back instructions • cannot remember sequence of instructions	• listens intently • can repeat back instructions • can remember a number of sequential instructions
Listening to stories	• looks round the room • asks apparently unrelated questions • engages in some other activity e.g. rolling up a bit of paper • talks to their peers	• listens intently • can answer questions about the story • can ask questions about the story • focuses on the task • becomes oblivious to everything round about
Listening to peers	• replies with an unrelated answer to a question • is not aware someone is speaking to them	• answers questions being asked • looks at their peers when they are talking
Watching	• lacks awareness • asks lower-order questions about pictures, e.g. 'Why is the boy crying in the picture?'	• looks for detail • asks higher-order questions, e.g. 'Why have the other children upset the boy in the picture?'

Writing

It would appear that humans have always sought to 'make a mark', for example through cave paintings and hieroglyphics. These 'marks' record for us 'life at the time'. In the 21st century our communication system relies heavily on the written as well as the spoken word, not to mention electronic communication.

From an early age most children become aware of the written word. They constantly see environmental print (e.g. road signs, shop names, the big 'M' for McDonalds). They may also see their parents, educators, siblings or relatives writing things down; for example, shopping lists, phone numbers, letters, reminders. Young children often try to copy adults and can be found 'making marks' on paper.

Often they can tell you exactly what these marks say. Children are already starting to make the connection between the written word and the conveying of meaning.

Resources: Paper, crayons, pencils, pens, chalk, chalkboards

Activity/resources	Responses	Advanced responses
Imaginative play, e.g. in the café/ shop; travel agent's; vet's; hospital; etc.	• enjoys scribbling but does not connect this to real-life situations • does not select an activity involving mark-making	• connects the marks they make with real-life situations • actively seeks out opportunities to 'practise' writing
'Have a go' writing table	• has to be encouraged to choose the activity • shows little interest in writing materials • shows little interest in communicating meaning through the written word • grasps the writing implement incorrectly	• enjoys making marks – real or pretend • can tell you what the 'writing' says • has a go at producing actual letters and numbers • grips the writing implement correctly • understands that groups of letters have meaning • asks 'how do you write…?'
Tracing	• cannot follow the lines • does not approach the task in a logical manner	• stays on the lines • selects an appropriate starting point and completes the task systematically
Following patterns	• lack of hand–eye coordination • does not start at the beginning of the pattern	• good hand–eye coordination • starts at the beginning and progresses logically

Reading

Undoubtedly there are some young children who quickly master the art of reading and arrive in the early years setting as competent readers. However, this decoding of print is only one aspect of reading. While this ability has to be challenged and developed, there are other aspects that are equally important:

• a love of books

• the pleasure that can be gained from reading

• the opportunity to 'hear' stories

• an understanding of their cultural past through nursery rhymes, fairy tales, etc.

• comprehension

• expression and intonation.

Reading, like the other activities identified, has to be seen in the wider context of literacy so that young children become confident communicators of thoughts and feelings as well as the mechanical process of 'reading'.

Resources: Books – fiction and non-fiction, leaflets, environmental print, e.g. notices, labels, computer

Activity/resources	Responses	Advanced responses
In the library corner	• seldom chooses to visit the library corner • flits from one book to the next without looking at them • fidgets and can't sit still during library time • does not participate in activity	• can be regularly found in the library corner • selects a book and gives reasons for doing so, e.g. 'I like the cover; I've read about this character before' • selects a book and studies it in detail • listens and engages in the activity
Retelling a story using a book	• retells story out of sequence • does not link up their story with the pictures on the page • turns pages apparently on a whim	• can retell story accurately • can retell the story using phrases from the book • turns pages at appropriate point • can read 'between the lines'
Handling a book	• holds the book upside-down • reads from back to front (although this is appropriate in some cultures) • does not follow text from left to right (also appropriate in some cultures) • struggles to turn pages • 'abuses' books, e.g. throws them, scrunches up pages, etc.	• knows how to hold a book • knows about technical details, e.g. cover, title, author, etc. • knows where the story starts • knows how to turn pages • can follow text from right to left • looks after books
Environmental print	• is unaware of environmental print • does not connect notices with particular behaviour, e.g. 'only 4 at the sand'	• asks what notices round the room say • attempts to 'read' the notices using clues to predict text • keen that notices round the room should be obeyed, e.g. 'only 4 at the sand'

Mathematics

Why mathematics?

• Mathematics is all around us and is an important part of everyday life.

• Mathematics can be creative and enjoyable.

• Mathematics can help us solve problems.

• There's a concern in the UK that children are not doing well at mathematics compared with those in other countries.

Perhaps mathematics more than any other subject is one people love to hate. Certainly large numbers of the population in the UK claim 'not to be good at mathematics'. This inability to 'do maths' is blamed on anything from poor teaching to fathers – 'my dad wasn't any good at maths either'. Somehow this is meant to make not being good at maths 'all right'. Often when considering mathematics we focus on one very narrow aspect – computation – in other words adding, subtracting, multiplying and dividing. Older children report that they do not like maths because it does not offer opportunities for creativity. And yet talk to anyone with a love of mathematics and they will tell you that maths is extremely creative. As educators we need to help children discover the joy of mathematics.

Let's think about the mathematical activities we offer in our early years setting. We will consider what we might see children doing during certain activities and we will also consider what children already proficient in particular skills will be doing. We will look at four common activities and their related resources in an early years setting:

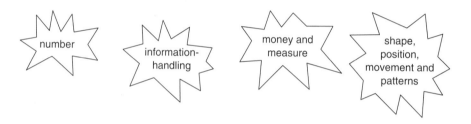

Number

Numbers are all around us in the early years setting, at home and in the community. Often activities in the early years setting do not relate directly to number but offer opportunities for young children to explore the nature and language of number. Placing the learning in a real-life context helps the child to see mathematics as a relevant aspect of life.

Resources: Cubes, beads, bricks, pictures, big books, the café, the shop

Activity/resources	Responses	Advanced responses
Recognising numerals, e.g. in pictures, imaginative play, etc.	• recognises significant numbers, e.g. age, house number • uses number names up to 10	• recognises a range of numbers in various contexts • uses number names beyond 10 • responds to the mathematical thinking of others
Counting, e.g. number of currants on buns	• miscounts/counts some buns twice • cannot count up to 10 consistently	• counts accurately • counts reliably up to 10 and beyond

Activity/resources	Responses	Advanced responses
Talking about adding on, taking away	• grasps the concept of one more/one less • grasps the concept of one more/one less but is reliant on concrete materials	• understands the concept of adding and subtracting • understands the concept of addition/subtraction in the abstract • can apply the concept within everyday situations, e.g. how many more cups do we need for snack time if there are 9 people in our group? • recognises the symbols for adding and subtracting

Shape, position, movement and patterns

Much of mathematics concerns patterns and how these relate to each other. Often in the early years setting this is restricted to recognising and re-creating patterns. We can help children to see patterns, to enjoy looking for them and to explore the relationships between shape, position, movement and number. The starting point for this should be an area of interest to the child, not some abstract task perhaps involving beads and string. Helping children to capture the enjoyment of mathematics must be key in what we do.

Resources: Jigsaws, puzzles

Activity/resources	Responses	Advanced responses
Jigsaws, puzzles	• does not turn pieces round when a piece won't fit • does not recognise the shape/colour of the piece is the same as the shape/colour of the space • does not see the 'big picture' • does not approach the task in a logical manner • becomes frustrated and gives up easily	• manipulates jigsaw pieces • can connect shape/colour of piece to shape/colour of space • knows what the final picture will be like • approaches the task logically, e.g. completes the corners first • connects the pieces with speed and ease
Positional language	• gets language of position muddled • cannot place objects in correct position	• uses language of position accurately • can follow instructions involving language of position • can give instructions using positional language
Identifying shapes	• gets names of 2D and 3D shapes muddled	• can name 2D and 3D shapes accurately • makes reference to properties of 2D and 3D shapes

(Continued)

(Continued)

Activity/resources	Responses	Advanced responses
Patterns and sequences	• inconsistent completion of patterns, e.g. copying Compare Bear sequence on a work card • misrepresentation of patterns • inability to recognise a pattern exists, e.g. becomes apparent through discussion	• copies patterns accurately • continues patterns • orally describes patterns

Information-handling

Making sense of the information round about us is a key skill. Learning to handle the information we gather is important if it is going to influence future decisions we make. Offering opportunities to record and interpret data is important. Supporting these skills in the early years is vital if we are to lay the foundations for future work.

Resources: Matrices, tree diagrams, the café

Activity/resources	Responses	Advanced responses
Sorting	• selects the most obvious way to sort • cannot articulate why they have selected that method • can only think of one way of sorting	• looks for imaginative ways of completing the task • offers more than one solution • offers more than one criterion for selection
Matrices and tree diagrams	• can sort on a matrix using one criterion • makes very little attempt to record, e.g. orders in the café	• can sort on a matrix using two or more criteria • able to identify own criteria for sorting • will record orders accurately in the café using own notation or making use of prepared charts or grids

Money and measure

In our modern world, many children never have the opportunity to handle money or to see money exchange hands. The following factors seem to have led to this situation:

• the use of credit and debit cards

• the demise of corner shops coupled with parents' fears about letting their children 'go to the shop'

• supermarkets where everything can be bought under one roof

- in schools, the rise of swipe-card cafeterias

- cost of items are beyond children's knowledge and experience of number (i.e. their number knowledge is 'up to 10' and most items cost more than this).

It is important therefore to offer opportunities within the early years setting for children to experience handling money.

Relating mathematical concepts to real life is crucial if children are going to see the relevance and meaning of activities in terms of life outside of education. Perhaps the most common mathematical activities we engage in outside of educational institutions are measuring and weighing.

Resources: The café, the shop, coins, songs, rhymes, rods, rulers, height charts

Activity/resources	Responses	Advanced responses
Handling money in the shop/café	• little concept of the value of different coins • little concept of different coins	• understands coins have different value • can identify different coins
Non-standard units of measurement	• has not grasped the importance of accuracy • will estimate but the estimate resembles a 'wild guess' • uses the language of measure in a limited way	• measures accurately • has grasped the importance of measuring accurately • is willing to estimate • estimates are reasonably accurate • has an understanding of the comparative nature of measure • uses the language of measure appropriately

The challenge now for the educator is how to take forward the learning of these individuals, ensuring that the 'whole child' is offered a chance to grow and develop. One common response to this challenge is to buy new resources. While new resources can be useful, in fact using the existing resources differently is often all that is required.

 Summing up

Some key points have been made in this chapter in relation to gifted and talented children's responses to resources and activities.

- The cross-curricular nature of problem-solving.
- The importance of developing thinking skills across the curriculum.
- The common resources and activities on offer across four specific curricular areas.
- The skills and abilities gifted and talented children might present in each of these curricular areas.

Useful websites

Exploratree: http://www.exploratree.org.uk

Futurelab's free online library of graphical 'thinking guides' – you can download them or fill them in and complete your project on the exploratree website.

Robert Fisher: http://www.teachingthinking.net/thinking/pages/robert_fisher_webresources.htm A selection of interesting articles on thinking skills.

Good Morning Children Ltd: http://www.goodmorningchildren.com/ For a small cost this site provides interactive whiteboard resources for the thinking classroom. Age range under 5 to 11+.

The TASC Wheel http://www.tascwheel.com/ A thinking skills framework.

Thinkers Keys is an exciting framework for the teaching of thinking. The Thinkers Keys feature 20 powerful strategies for generating quality intellectual rigour in every-day classroom practice. Some resources are free at: http://www.thinkerskeys.com/

Further reading

Taggart, G., Ridley, K., Rudd, P. and Benefield, P. (2005) *Thinking Skills in the Early Years: A Literature Review.* Slough: NFER.

Wallace, B. (2002) *Teaching Thinking Skills Across the Early Years: A Practical Approach for Children Aged 4 to 7.* London: NACE/Fulton Publishers.

Walsh, G., Murphy, P. and Dunbar, C. (2007) *Thinking Skills in the Early Years: A guide for practitioners.* (written in collaboration with Early Years Enriched Curriculum Evaluation Project Team.) Available as a PDF at: http://www.nicurriculum.org.uk/docs/skills_and_capabilities/foundation/ThinkingSkillsintheEarlyYears_Report.pdf (accessed September 2011).

Physical movement/motor development

This chapter will:

> - **Consider why it is important to develop and challenge the skills young children display in physical movement/motor development.**
> - **Offer some activities to challenge young children in their learning.**

As suggested in Chapter 3, many young children will already have well-developed skills in this area and so the early years educator needs to consider how they will develop and challenge these skills in an inclusive framework. Each child has a right to a challenging learning experience, and the area of physical movement and motor development is no exception.

However, we need to guard against identifying and hot-housing young children who show particular ability. The Scottish Sports' Council recently said that early identification is not always a good thing. Indeed, it can lead to children reaching a plateau and may in fact hinder them from becoming sportsmen and women in the future. Young muscles and skeletons have to be allowed to form and develop without being damaged. Getting the balance between early identification of particular abilities and appropriate challenge at the right level is not easy. Perhaps it brings us once again to the notion that in early years we should be focusing on offering challenging opportunities and next steps. The temptation for educators may be to introduce structured games and activities – however, the activities suggested here are not about how to produce the next world-class athletes but they are about helping young children first and foremost to enjoy movement, which, of course, may be the start of their journey towards becoming a world-class athlete. Proprioception refers to the body's ability to sense movement, which, of course, mey be the steet of their journey towards becoming a world-class athlete. This ability enables us to know where our limbs are in space without having to look. It will help us to know how close we are to others or objects. It is important in everyday activities but especially so in complicated sporting movements, where precise coordination is essential. Linked to this is awareness of balance and movement. This is connected to the vestibular system which monitors movement. Children will often spin around until they are dizzy and then try to walk in a straight line. Of course they can't because the messages from the middle ear are muddled. It is the vestibular system that monitors whether we are sitting or standing, the position of our head, and so on. Opportunities to find out about our bodies abound in an early years setting – climbing, running, rolling, spinning, twisting, going up and down stairs are all part of understanding how our bodies work. While we can develop mastery of our bodies within the activities in this chapter, understanding our sense of self crosses curricular areas and can be developed through activities in music and art, and initiatives such as Forest Schools (see Chapter 8). Developing a good sense of movement and balance will impact on our readiness for other activities such as reading. Good practice in this area will:

- develop existing skills
- help children to transfer skills they already possess from one situation to another
- offer new physical movement and motor development opportunities
- help children of all abilities to work together
- help children to enjoy moving

So where do we start?

Challenging activities

Climbing

Resource: Climbing apparatus

Activity/resources	Advanced responses	Possible challenging activities
Climbing, e.g. on apparatus	• have confidence on apparatus • hold body weight with ease • display effortless, flowing movements as they climb • use opposite arm/leg action • have a strong grasp of the bars	1. climb vertically using different parts of the body differently or climb horizontally using different parts of the body differently 2. create a problem-solving type activity

1   An adult should supervise these activities. Start by explaining what the words 'vertical' and 'horizontal' mean. Ask the children if they can think of animals that move horizontally and vertically. They might, for example, suggest a snake and a chimpanzee. Have a collection of pictures ready for the children to look at and identify whether they show people, animals or objects moving vertically or horizontally. Ask the children to climb up the climbing frame but suggest that they can only use certain parts of their body. For example, they could use:

- hands only

- right hand and left leg only

- left hand and right leg only

- different kinds of grips.

2   Link the work you do at the climbing frame to your topic work. For example, if you are learning about the sea you could:

-   put a piece of blue material under the climbing frame

-   explain to the children that the climbing frame is a desert island and they are stranded on the island

-   tell them that if they can reach the top of the island they will find food and water and they will be able to wave for help

-   tell them they can climb around the apparatus, over the apparatus and along the apparatus but that they must not fall off because sharks swim in the sea around the island (alternatively, tell them they can only climb around the apparatus, they are not allowed to go over it, along it or through it)

-   add a further challenge by linking up two children with a short length of rope, like mountain climbers, and ask them to reach the top of the island together. **This activity would need close adult supervision.**

This kind of work on the climbing frame can be carried over to art and design work, for example, where the children might paint or make a model of their escape from the island.

Running

Resource: Large spaces

Activity/resources	Advanced responses	Possible challenging activities
Running	<ul><li>bent forwards</li><li>flowing action</li><li>leg and arm movements in opposition to each other</li><li>head up</li><li>during the running process the runner is in the air</li><li>the supporting leg is firm and extended</li></ul>	1. explore changes of direction 2. consider different kinds of running 3. run in different paths 4. run in relation to obstacles or people

1   Children need to explore how their running changes according to the amount of space they have. They also need to be aware of direction as they run. Even children who have a strong running action need to know how to harness this ability and use it to their advantage. Ask the children to run in different directions:

-   forwards

-   backwards

- sideways

- in circles.

Change the space you offer the children. You could have:

- a large space

- a small space

- an unusually shaped space

- a large space with obstacles in it

- a small space with obstacles in it

- an unusually shaped space with obstacles in it.

2   Children also need to be aware of different types of running. Ask them to:

- run like an angry wild animal

- run like a balloon floating in the air

- run a short distance very quickly

- run a longer distance at a slower pace.

3   Having explored changes of direction, space and different kinds of running, children now need to be able to run in specific pathways. You could:

- set out skittles and ask the children to run between them

- lay out hoops and ask the children to run from the red one to the blue one, etc.

- ask the children to run round the room visiting particular corners or features in a particular order

- ask the children to make up their own path for running

- have the children make up pathways for others.

4   Learning to run in relation to obstacles or people will be an important skill for later when games skills are introduced. Learning the basics of these skills in a non-competitive setting and in relation to the activities above will support children in their development and learning. You could:

- ask the children to sidestep each other as they run round the room

- roll a large ball across the room and ask the children to sidestep it

- ask the children to run in pairs with one chasing the other; they have to sidestep each other as they run

- ask the children to keep running at the same pace as they sidestep an object or a person.

Throwing and catching

Resources: Large balls, beanbags, small balls, quoits

Activity/resources	Advanced responses	Possible challenging activities
Throwing, e.g. overarm throw Catching	• arm swings back prior to throw • weight transfers forwards • non-throwing arm is held out to aid balance • steps forward on opposite foot to throwing arm • throwing arm follows through towards the direction of the throw • uses forearms with elbows bent to catch a ball efficiently and securely	1. use a variety of objects when throwing 2. throwing for distance 3. throwing for accuracy 4. have the child be aware of body movements as they throw 5. decrease the size of the ball

1   Children should be exposed to a variety of appropriate objects for throwing. A useful discussion can ensue as to what is or is not appropriate. Common objects to be found in an early years setting include:

- balls of various sizes and made from various materials (see below)

- quoits

- foam javelins

- beanbags

- frisbees

- foam darts.

A variety of balls should be provided that will not only develop traditional skills but will also develop sensory awareness. These might include:

- balls that are stress relievers and are soft and squidgy

- porcupine balls or flame balls that are tactile and have dozens of stretchy tentacles all over

- XaXa juggling balls that allow you to change the weight and colour combinations (shell and skin) and the sound

- koosh balls that are made of rubber filaments attached to a soft rubber core and get their name from the sound they make when they land

- disco glide ball – a black ball within a transparent ball that glides effortlessly along without rolling

- tangle ball made from multi-coloured interwoven links. It bounces, is easy to catch and can be unwound.

2   Discuss with the children the idea of throwing something a distance. Children can suggest a time when throwing something a distance would be useful. Pictures of people throwing things, e.g. javelin throwing, shot put, etc. can be cut out of magazines or newspapers or found on the internet. More unusual throwing events can be displayed and discussed, e.g. welly-throwing or tossing the caber at a Highland Games. Allow the children the opportunity to experiment with throwing objects a distance. Children can find out the shape of object that is easier to throw or travels furthest. Children should be encouraged to try out a range of throws:

- underarm

- overarm

- sideways.

They should also be encouraged to throw objects different distances, increasing in length as the child progresses. They should also become aware of what kind of throw is best for the task. For example, which kind of throw is best if we want to:

- throw for speed

- throw for accuracy

- throw to let someone hit it with a bat

- throw to hit a target?

3   Accurate throwing is important, for safety among other things. Offering children the opportunity to throw for accuracy will help them to develop their already evident abilities and skills. You should:

- set up a target for the children to aim for or let the children select a target

- increase the distance between the child and the target

- increase or decrease the height of the target

- ask the child to stand inside a hoop when they throw

- make the target a moving target

- use a variety of objects to hit the target

- add challenges, e.g. can they hit the target if they close one eye, are blindfolded, stand with their back to the target, throw the object between their legs?

4 Children with ability will often almost naturally move their bodies in a particular way when throwing. Pointing out why they are throwing with accuracy can be helpful when the child starts to refine these movements even further.

- Talk with the child about the position their body is in as they throw.

- Encourage the child to change their body positions.

- Ask the child to explain why the object hits the target when they stand a particular way.

5 The balls being thrown should decrease in size. Children should be encouraged to catch the ball to the side of their body space. They should also be throwing a ball in the air and catching it.

Jumping

Resource: Flat space

Activity/resources	Advanced responses	Challenging activities
Jumping, e.g. a vertical jump	<ul><li>squat down prior to jumping</li><li>legs extend and stretch</li><li>body is fully stretched when in the air</li><li>controlled landing with knees and ankles bent</li></ul>	1. explore different kinds of landing 2. jump for height 3. jump for distance 4. combine activities 5. problem-solving activities

1 Jumping should only take place on soft surfaces such as mats or grass. Landing after a jump is an important part of the jump itself. Once the child can land comfortably on two feet, they should be asked to:

- land on one foot

- land crouched down

- land on two feet in a balanced position

- land on one foot in a balanced position.

2 Children should be encouraged to jump for height. This is another skill that can be developed once the child is older and participating in structured games, e.g. netball, volleyball. Children should be asked to:

- burst into the air from a crouched position

- explode into the air and land in a different place from the starting position

- use their arms to propel them into the air

- experiment taking off and landing on one foot and two feet and deciding which one thrusts them higher into the air.

3   As well as propelling themselves into the air when jumping, jumping for distance can also be developed. Ask the children to:

- take off from two feet and land further forward on one foot

- take off from one foot and land further forward on two feet

- jump and land in a diagonal position from where they started

- jump as far as they can.

4   Combining activities and movements offers children the opportunity to use their imaginations and to think creatively. Explain that they can combine any of the jumping movements they can do to make a sequence. Children could:

- jump, turn round in the air and land

- combine two kinds of jumps, e.g. one jump for height and one for distance

- jump off a piece of apparatus, e.g. a bench, and see how far they can go before landing

- hop a distance then jump for height.

5   As with the climbing frame, it's probably best to integrate this kind of activity with your topic work. For example, if you were learning about the jungle:

- Each child selects an animal they have been learning about.

- Hoops can be laid out on the floor.

- Each hoop represents a tree top.

- A bench can be set out to represent the animal's den.

- Children have to reach their den by jumping into each of the hoops.

- The hoops can be laid out in varying measures apart.

- Children should be encouraged to explore using a range of jumps. This would include experimenting with take-offs and landings.

- To add extra challenge the children could pick up items from each hoop that have to be delivered safely to the den. You could use beanbags, foam balls, etc., as the objects to be collected.

Using a bat and ball

Resources: Various size balls, various size bats

Activity/resources	Advanced responses	Challenging activities
Using a bat and ball	<ul><li>bat is in position to receive the ball</li><li>body faces the side in preparation</li><li>weight is moved to front foot</li><li>eyes follow the ball through the air</li><li>bat hits ball with sweeping action</li></ul>	1. use varying sizes of equipment 2. hit the ball in a variety of ways 3. vary the trajectory of the ball 4. use the bat to direct the ball through obstacles

1 Varying the size of equipment will help the child to refine and hone their skills and abilities. You can use:

- large balls, small bat

- small balls, large bat

- a cricket bat

- a baseball bat

- a tennis racquet

- a table-tennis bat

- footballs

- foam balls

- tennis balls

- plastic lightweight balls.

Children can be encouraged to explore and record the differences that the different types of bats and balls make.

2 When children are hitting accurately, they can be challenged by asking them to:

- tap the ball gently

- hit the ball hard

- hit the ball in a particular direction

- hit the ball so that it lands and bounces in a hoop.

3   Tying in with point 2 above, children can be asked to:

- hit the ball so that it makes a large arc in the sky

- hit the ball so that it skims across the floor

- hit the ball so that it goes in a straight line from the bat

- hit the ball so that it arcs before it bounces.

4   Being able to hit the ball with some degree of accuracy is a skill that will be beneficial as structured games are played later on. Experimenting with a bat, ball and objects at this stage will allow the children to:

- develop hand–eye coordination

- estimate distance and speed

- understand the need for accuracy when hitting the ball.

The room can be set up with different obstacles laid out. For example:

- rows of skittles could be placed in a twisting pathway

- skittles and canes can be set up in a pathway.

---

1   If your early years setting has access to the school gym hall, arrange to meet with an older class. Organise the children into groups so that an older child and a younger child are working together. The older child can act as a 'buddy' to the younger child. Together they can explore:

- ways of travelling across the floor or equipment together

- ways of rolling across mats

- bat-and-ball activities

- running activities.

As well as having an impact on physical movement, the teaming up of younger children with older children also allows friendships to develop and often these friendships are carried on into the playground or school yard where incidents of bullying can be lessened as children learn to communicate with one another and care for one another.

2   Find out what sports competitions are on, for example the Olympic Games, the Winter Olympics, the Commonwealth Games, Marathons, gymnastics, The World Cup – host your own version of these events. Children can be encouraged to improve their own personal best times.

As well as offering an opportunity to develop physical skills, these events offer wonderful opportunities for inter-disciplinary and cross-curricular learning.

3 If you have access to a sports coordinator or a local sports team/coach invite them in to work with you and the children. Remember that children may also have well developed fine motor skills with the use of the thumb and little finger and the arches of their hands well established and a preferred hand being determined. The two hands will be able to execute different movements at the same time. This means they will be able to pick up a number of small objects in one hand, fold paper, draw more accurately, etc. Activities that demand fine dexterity can be introduced, such as knitting, embroidery, weaving, making small models, creating mosaics or pottery.

4 Explore different kinds of dance including traditional and folk dancing. This will encourage balance, rhythm, coordination, sequencing of steps and, of course, offers opportunities to find out more about the countries and traditions the dances come from, the music that accompanies them, etc.

5 Watch out for any free sporting events children could attend to either participate in or watch. Children can also watch extracts of sporting events on TV to find out more about the skills required for their chosen sport.

6 Invite members from local sports teams and groups to come and talk to the children. They could cover aspects such as training, healthy eating, perseverance, goal setting, practice.

Many of these activities are adult-led. For an even richer learning experience ask the children to help you devise these.

Summing up

Some key points and suggestions have been made in this chapter in relation to challenging activities in the area of physical and motor development. They include:

- the importance of developing and challenging the skills young children display in physical movement/motor development
- some activities to challenge young children in their learning.

Useful websites

BBC website: http://www.bbc.co.uk/schools/primaryhistory/ancient_greeks/the_olympic_games/ This website contains interesting information about the history of the Olympic Games.

Folk dancing: http://www.earlychildhoodnews.com/earlychildhood/article_view.aspx?ArticleID=301 This website contains some helpful information about teaching folk dancing to young children.

Sensory Fun: http://sensoryfun.com/sensory_integration_activities.htm This website contains fun ideas for developing proprioceptive and vestibular abilities.

Scottish Ballet: http://connect.scottishballet.co.uk/ This website allows children to explore behind the scenes at the ballet.

Further reading

Woodfield, L. (2004) *Physical Development in the Early Years.* London: Continuum International Publishing Group.

5

Music

This chapter will:

- **Consider why it is important to develop and challenge the skills young children display in music.**
- **Offer some activities to challenge young children in their learning.**

There is no doubt that child prodigies exist. However, to suggest that musical ability only lies within a few would not give us a true picture of the breadth of musical talent that exists in our early years settings. Unquestionably some children arrive at our early years setting having had a rich musical experience and will often display signs of early ability in music. These children and their abilities must be challenged and developed. Nonetheless, one of the fundamental arguments in this book is that children need to develop in a rounded way and so to focus purely on the development of their musical abilities at the expense of others may well be detrimental to their overall development. Other children within the setting may be equally capable of demonstrating such musical ability but the lack of opportunity to explore their musicality has been denied them and so it is important that opportunity is available for all. Opportunity, experimenting, confidence, interest and practice all seem to contribute to musical development and so it is with these ideas in mind that activities have been developed. It is worth noting that the confidence of the adults in the setting will impact on the opportunities offered to children. It is important that children see adults engaging in music making and so all adults in the setting should be encouraged to participate. Just as we might scaffold children's learning, adults can be supported through:

- working alongside a more confident individual

- learning the song in advance so you can sing it more confidently. Using a backing CD can help here as it will keep you in tune and on time

- learning alongside the children as they explore and make music with instruments and their voices

- keeping practising – you will become more confident!

Harrison and Pound (1996) carried out a study in which they considered the early experiences of successful musicians. They identified nine elements that were important:

1   The musicians usually grew up in a musical environment.

2   From an early age they heard and saw music as part of everyday life.

3   Many of the adults with whom they came into contact were musically active.

4   It was expected that all children would develop as musicians.

5   They often had informal access to instruments.

6   They had time to explore both the expressive and technical possibilities of the instruments.

7   They were allowed to join in the general music-making.

8   They had early opportunities for playing and singing alongside others with a variety of expertise.

9   The initial emphasis in their music-making was on enjoyment rather than on acquiring technical skill. (Harrison and Pound, 1996: 235)

By carefully constructing a musically rich environment early years settings can nurture ability and offer enjoyable opportunities for all. Developing teacher confidence in music is important

Challenging activities

Singing

Resources: Nursery rhymes, action songs, counting songs, echo songs, tapes, CDs

Activity/resources	Advanced responses	Possible challenging activities
Singing a song. 'Okki Tokki Unga': Action Songs for Children; Apusskidu: Songs for Children; Mango Spice: 44 Caribbean Songs; Tongo: Count Me In: 44 Songs and Rhymes about Numbers; Tom Thumb's Musical Maths: Developing Maths Skills with Simple Songs; etc.	• enthusiastic • responds to activities • can hold a tune • makes up songs • enjoys performing • recognises familiar songs in varying contexts, e.g. on TV • follow contours of a melody	1. offer opportunities for informal singing 2. make a book about their favourite songs 3. ask the child to teach the group/ adults a song 4. develop actions for songs 5. begin using invented notation 6. start singing two- and three-part songs 7. select songs that allow for dynamics and extension of vocal range

1   As children move around the early years setting, encourage them to take part in spontaneous singing. This can happen in any area of the early years setting and can happen indoors or out of doors or when engaging in another task. This is important for building up creativity in music. If the singing occurs outdoors, it is a good place to explore dynamics – How loud can you sing? How softly can you sing? Children can also be asked to sing their song in a particular style:

   • Country and Western

   • opera

   • jazz

   • boy-band

   • lullaby.

2   Children are likely to have built up a repertoire of their favourite songs. Ask them to produce pictures about their song to make into a book for others to use. Have the children illustrate the book. This offers the opportunity for developing language – written, musical and spoken – and encourages children to:

   • think about the words they are singing

   • think about the meaning the song conveys

   • use music as a stimulus for creative art work.

3   If children are holding a tune well of a song they know, and if they have confidence, ask them to teach the group and/or the adults the song. This offers wonderful opportunities for the children to:

   • engage in leader–chorus activities where the child is the leader

   • feel that their musical knowledge is respected and valued

   • listen to the sounds being produced by themselves and others.

4   If the children can sing a song unfamiliar to the early years setting, actions can be devised to go with the song by:

   • the children themselves

   • the adult

   • the other children in the group

   • acting out the meaning of the words

   • listening to the pattern of the tune, e.g. when the tune 'goes up'/'gets higher', the action 'goes up'/'gets higher', etc.

5   The adult can work with the child in creating a written response in the form of invented notations for the song they are singing. 'Notation' is the name given to pictorial representations that will help children to develop an awareness of musical structures and conventions. These invented notations might include:

- lines

- curls

- squiggles

- a combination of symbols and pictures.

6   When the child is sustaining a tune, then two- and three-part songs and rounds can be introduced. This allows the child to:

- be part of a collective singing group

- begin to hear and identify harmonies.

7   Songs that offer opportunities to develop vocal control should be selected. Songs that allow children to increase and then decrease in volume and songs that allow them to extend their vocal range should be sung. Long sustained notes can be practised. Staff should note it is important to allow children to sing accompanied as well as unaccompanied. Adult voices can be of a low pitch and continually singing unaccompanied like this will not encourage children to explore and sing high notes accurately.

Instruments and sound-making

Resources: Tuned percussion instruments, e.g. chime bars, hand chimes, piano; untuned percussion, e.g. drums, woodblocks, bells, shakers, triangles, cymbals, tambourines

Activity/resources	Advanced responses	Challenging activities
Instruments and sound-making	<ul><li>remembers how to hold and play the instrument</li><li>has control over their movements when playing</li><li>can play as part of a group at appropriate times</li><li>can pick out a tune on an instrument</li><li>can echo rhythms</li></ul>	1. develop a musical 'conversation' between the adult and the child or between children 2. encourage children to play instruments in response to other children's movements 3. encourage children to play instruments for other children to respond to in their movements 4. organise band sessions where the child is the conductor

Activity/resources	Advanced responses	Challenging activities
Keeping the beat using untuned percussion instruments	• keeps regular beat • strong control of movements • can vary pace • can tap back simple rhythms • can make up simple rhythms	5. record the child playing instruments 6. start to make connections between sounds and mark-making, e.g. follow simple pictorial notation 7. encourage loud music-making
Dynamics, e.g. high/low; fast/slow; loud/soft	• can differentiate sounds • can select appropriate dynamic for a situation, e.g. loud for a storm	8. string together sounds to create a story or sound picture

1   Developing musical 'conversations' can involve the adult in music-making alongside the child or the child in music-making alongside a peer or older child. In each case the lead comes from the child. This kind of musical conversation includes:

- using tuned percussion instruments to mimic the child

- using untuned percussion instruments to mimic the child

- using parts of the body, e.g. shoulders, knees, elbows, to respond to the child's rhythm

- allowing the child to play the rhythm with the partner playing it back.

2   As their peers are moving about the early years setting or are in the gym, the child can respond to this movement by:

- selecting and playing an appropriate instrument to accompany the movement

- asking the children to move according to the type of instrument selected, e.g. bells suggest light movements, two-tone wood block suggests hopping, stilted movements

- using instruments and voice to accompany the children's movement.

3   Have the child select a range of instruments. As they play the instruments, have their peers move around the early years setting or gym in a way that reflects the sounds they hear. This could be connected to topic work; for example, if discussing the weather, the child could select instruments that reflect a storm, a sunny day, a cold day, etc.

4   Organise 'orchestra' sessions (this could be with older children as well as age peers) during which the children play instruments, with the children and adults taking turns to be the conductor. Children should be encouraged to experiment with signals as they conduct the 'orchestra'.

5   Record the children as they play. This allows the children and the adults to:

- hear the sound they produce

- accompany themselves on the CD, thus multi-layering the sounds they create

- discuss the sounds created

- return to the music at a later date

- use the created music as a stimulus for art work, creative writing

- explore nature

- devise a sound picture.

6   A range of instruments – tuned, untuned and homemade – should be available and children should be encouraged to explore the sounds these make. Discussing with the child the shape of the sounds, words that describe the sounds and what the sound sounds like will help them to:

- begin to visualise a written mark that corresponds to the sound

- experiment with shapes on paper and sounds produced

- read the marks and be able to reproduce a sound at a later date.

7   Opportunities to play with a range of untuned and tuned percussion instruments should be offered and children can also experiment by making sounds with objects found in the setting. Children should be encouraged to make loud music. Outdoors offers great opportunities for loud music making and also encourages children to explore sounds made by nature, for example the rain, wind in the trees, etc. While large musical instruments can be expensive, e.g. large cymbals, settings can easily create music making areas by stringing up household objects such as pots and pans, frying pans and lids for children to 'play'. Plastic buckets and drain pipes can be used for exploring sound making and hollow plastic tubes can be stuck into the ground and used like drums. Settings may also have wind chimes in the outdoor area and these can be utilised too.

8   Using a selection of instruments (as described in point 6 above), children can create sounds to accompany a story. This story can be a well-known tale or one that the children have written themselves. Building on experimenting with sounds, the children can start to create moods by:

- selecting an appropriate instrument to create the effect they desire

- altering the response to the story by playing softly, loudly, etc.

- altering the response by changing the tone, e.g. using a different beater

- beginning to associate music with feelings and moods and recognising that these can alter.

Using the selection of instruments or parts of their body children can write their own musical score for a story. For example:

- Tell the children they are caught in a storm and the rain is starting. Ask what instrument or body sound would depict this.

- Once they have decided on the most appropriate instrument/sound ask them what that would look like and record this on a large piece of paper.

- Build up the picture of the storm by adding the wind, hailstones, gentler breeze, sunshine, etc.

By the end you should have a written score which the children can 'read' and perform. This score can be kept and added to at a later date, and of course this helps to secure the idea that the written word can be returned to and adapted. It also offers the opportunity for children with musical ability to make links to formal musical notation and musical symbols.

Music appreciation

Resources: CDs, tapes, DVDs, sound tracks

Activity/resources	Advanced responses	Challenging activities
Listening to a piece of music, e.g. Peter and the Wolf, Debussy, music from non-Western culture	• offers an emotional response • sways in time to the music • recognises the music, e.g. 'that sounds like...' • can equate a time/place/ event with the music • can re-create the music, e.g. through singing, playing the rhythms, etc. later • asks to hear favourite pieces of music • asks to hear new pieces of music	1. offer a range of listening material 2. provide an area with instruments, ribbons and other props for responding to music 3. link listening to music to other curricular areas, e.g. art, story corner 4. take time to talk to the child about their music preferences 5. use spoken language to respond to music 6. create an environmental map of sound 7. invite musicians – professionals, parents, older children – to play for the children 8. show pictures to the children and ask them to identify music that would suit the mood of the picture

1   It is important that children have the opportunity to hear a range of music. A music library should be built up and should include a variety of types of music. Children can be encouraged to bring in their favourite CDs from home. The variety should include:

- jazz

- rhythm and blues

- rap

- opera

- Country and Western

- orchestral

- electronically produced music

- steel band

- African drumming music

- house music

- string quartet

- choir music.

2   Alongside the listening corner should be an area that allows children to respond in a physical and concrete way to the music they are hearing. Instruments, ribbons, paper and crayons, scarves, strips of material can be available. Children should be encouraged to:

- explore ways of using the props to demonstrate their understanding of the music

- select the appropriate prop for the kind of music being played, e.g. a ribbon floating to denote light, airy music

- colour or draw what the music is suggesting to them.

3   An extension of the work suggested above is to explicitly connect the music to other curricular areas. A deliberate linking of subjects by the adult will allow children to explore:

- the cross-curricular nature of music

- the cross-curricular nature of learning

- the importance of the transfer of skills from one setting to another.

The links between mathematics and music are well known, but equally music links to the development of rhythm which is important for reading, the exploration and development of emotions which supports personal development, understanding countries and cultures through listening to traditional music and learning about traditional instruments.

4   Helping children to articulate what it is they like about particular music and why it is they like it, helps the children to feel valued and allows the educator to enter the world of the children as they listen to music. It is important to:

- accept the reasons the children present for liking/disliking particular music

- accept that musical tastes are different for different people

- allow children to explore their feelings and fears through music

- acknowledge that music is a very powerful and emotive tool

- explore cultures through listening to different music.

5   Music can be used as a stimulus for language development. Listening to a variety of music will allow the educator and child to:

- explore words to explain sounds

- translate feelings into words

- broaden vocabulary through music

- investigate the relationship between words and nonsense words as the children describe what they are hearing.

6   Going for a walk around the early years setting and listening to the everyday sounds will allow you to build up an environmental 'sound map'. This encourages children to:

- listen for detail

- listen for natural sounds

- listen for repeated pattern sounds

- devise ways of recoding these sounds symbolically to share with others.

7   For many people nothing can compare to hearing live music. Invite professional musicians, parents who play an instrument or older children who play an instrument to your early years setting to play and talk about their instrument. This allows children to:

- hear first-hand about an instrument

- see an instrument close up

- hear the tone and volume of an instrument for themselves

- find out about different families of instruments, i.e. string, woodwind, brass, percussion

- play along on instruments with a live musician

- sing with a live accompaniment.

8   Show the children different genres of art work – have the children select music to match the pictures. Gifted and talented pupils will be able to work with more complex art work and music but it is a good idea to start off with more straightforward ideas that relate to feelings – happy, sad, angry, etc.

1 As part of your themed work, work with the children to:

- write a story line for a play

- write a script for your story line

- compose songs for your script

- compose a sound picture to accompany your script and songs

- make instruments to use as part of the sound picture

- make costumes and masks for the play

- choreograph the play

- rehearse your work

- perform the play for older children, parents, the community.

This will challenge the child with abilities but, equally importantly, it will be good fun and a learning experience for all.

2 When a child is displaying particularly advanced ability, the setting can seek advice from musical staff, parents, music teachers and professional musicians as how best to develop the abilities demonstrated.

3 Some children will benefit from hearing and seeing live performances. Being able to talk to the musician about their instrument/s, composing, etc. will allow them to ask more technical questions. Find out if any musicians are connected to the area or if any parents are musical. Invite them into the setting to talk about what they do and answer any questions. Allow them to spend time with individuals who are showing particular interest or ability in music and performance.

4 Make sure all styles of music are listened to and valued within the setting. This includes music from other cultures and countries and listening to pop as well as classical music.

5 Encourage and if possible attend live performances of different genres of music. Find out if there are any free musical performances in your area and arrange to take children to them, e.g. music festivals or competitions.

Many of these activities are adult-led. For an even richer learning experience ask the children to help you devise these.

Summing up

Some key points and suggestions have been made in this chapter in relation to challenging activities in the area of music.
They include:

- the importance of developing and challenging the skills young children display in music
- some activities to challenge young children in their learning.

Useful websites

BBC schools radio: http://www.bbc.co.uk/schoolradio/music/ The early years section contains a range of materials for use.

Fischy Music: http://www.fischy.com/ supports emotional, social and spiritual health and well-being in children through songs.

Music Express: http://www.acblack.com/musicexpress/ This site comprises everything needed to implement curriculum music and is fully accessible to non-music readers.

New York Philharmonic Kids: http://www.nyphilkids.org/lockerroom/main.phtml has some good ideas for music-making which could be adapted for early years. Adults could also work alongside children as they play some of the games.

Out of the Ark Song Books: http://www.outoftheark.co.uk/?dest=UK A range of resources for 3–11-year-olds including songs for assemblies, musicals and nativities. They come with an accompaniment CD for rehearsals and performances.

San Francisco Kids: http://www.sfskids.org/templates/splash.asp are committed to music education, within their community and beyond. This site would allow adults to work alongside children as they explore instruments, the orchestra, etc.

Sing Up! http://www.singup.org The group want to place singing at the heart of every school child's life, because they believe singing can change lives and build stronger communities. The website is full of downloadable backing tracks, lesson plans, etc.

Teaching Drums: http://www.teachingdrums.com/ provides African educational workshops for schools, colleges, universities and youth groups in the UK. The website provides a range of interesting ideas and information which can be used in the early years setting.

Further reading

Japp, A. (2009) *A Little Class Music: A Practical Guide for Non-specialist Primary Teachers.* Glasgow: Scottish Network for Able Pupils. Can be ordered from: www.ablepupils.com

Pound, L. and Harrison, C. (2003) *Supporting Musical Development in the Early Years.* Buckingham: Open University Press.

Young, S. (2008) *Music 3–5.* Abingdon: Routledge.

Literacy and language

This chapter will:

> - **Consider why it is important to develop and challenge the skills young children display in literacy and language.**
> - **Offer some activities to challenge young children in their learning.**

Within the early years setting, 'literacy' is often an umbrella term for talking, reading, writing and listening. Remember that thinking is also part of this equation but we looked at that in Chapter 3 as it is crucial to early years development. It is often the extremely articulate child who 'stands out' in an early years setting. They communicate in a way, on a level and use vocabulary that their peers do not. Similarly a child who can read is sometimes taken to be gifted and talented. While it is important to challenge and recognise these abilities, the early years educator must be careful not to confuse precocious speech or early reading with outstanding linguistic and literacy ability.

We should be aiming for a wide and rich literacy experience that ensures all children have the opportunity to develop, and:

- play with words

- come into contact with the social nature of language

- make marks for meaning

- enter the world of print

- learn to appreciate others' viewpoints.

Developing these wide-ranging literacy skills will help the child to develop linguistically. They will not simply become 'better readers' or more articulate individuals.

When thinking about literacy educators should:

- develop existing skills

- help children to transfer skills they already possess from one situation to another

- offer new language-rich opportunities taking account of media developments

- help children of all abilities to work together

- help children to enjoy literacy.

Challenging activities

Talking

Resources: Books, pictures, games, artwork, circle time, snack time

Activity/resources	Advanced responses	Challenging activities
Retelling a story	• recounts story sequentially • recounts the story with accurate details • 'reads between the lines' • predicts the outcome from the clues so far • uses adjectives • can create an atmosphere	1. develop story-telling skills 2. act out the story
Recounting an experience	• recounts events precisely • uses expression to make a point • will talk about others as well as themselves	3. create a narrative about themselves
Communicating with peers	• initiates conversation • interacts and engages in the conversation • elaborates on the topic	4. develop conversations with peers
Explaining something, e.g. their art work	• uses adjectives • gives reasons for their response • can give a personal reason for their response	5. talking with peers and adults

1   Children should be encouraged to develop story-telling skills alongside retelling stories. This is quite different from telling a story through reading a book. To develop these skills you should:

- encourage the children to think of a storyline beforehand: what exciting things will happen in the story; how will they communicate that to their audience; how will the story finish?

- encourage the children to listen to the sounds of the words as they say them. They should include nonsense words, rhyming words, unusual words. Spoken language should be fun!

- suggest that repeated phrases in a story means that their peers can join in the story-telling

- help the children to develop different voices for different characters. This will help their audience relate to the characters.

At first the stories will be quite short. This is OK. Stories will expand and develop as the story-teller becomes familiar and secure in the art of story-telling.

2   Favourite stories can be acted out with props. The props can be made by the children and/or educator or can be gathered specifically for the purpose. The acting out of the story allows the children to explore and experiment with voice production. The re-creation of well-known stories is important in the development of story structure and language. It offers opportunities to expand vocabulary and to make up fun, rhyming words.

3   While retelling a familiar story is important, it is also important to help children to develop 'personal narratives'. In other words, they should create a story about themselves. This is not a fantasy type of story but a real account of their lives. Children should be encouraged to share with others significant things that are happening in their lives. For example, if a child has a birthday they can tell their peers about the birthday celebrations; they can show how much they have grown and developed since their last birthday; they can consider how much they have changed since they were born. Significant achievements in the early years setting and beyond can be discussed so that a full biographical picture can emerge. This acknowledgement of them as a person will contribute to their sense of identity and will help them to feel part of the learning community to which they belong.

4   Children who are gifted and talented can often communicate extremely well with adults but struggle to communicate with their age peers. The early years setting offers wonderful opportunities for developing communication:

Play. Carefully constructed role-play or problem-solving or problem-finding situations can encourage children to communicate and engage in collaborative play. When children are inclined to play alone or in parallel play (as often gifted and talented children are) then the role of the adult is crucial in ensuring that collaborative play happens. Gentle guidance and careful questioning for opinions or thoughts by the adult can become the link between the children. This helps children to consider others' opinions and feelings and can help them to begin to connect to the others around them even when they appear to think differently.

Role-play with 'expert adults' allows us to capitalise on their ability to communicate with adults. For example, an orthopaedic nurse working in the hospital corner brought technical knowledge and vocabulary to the role-play that I was not able to provide. She also helped the children to build 'real-life' junk model hospital equipment. Working with these children in the hospital corner and during the art and craft activity allowed her to discuss how equipment works, how bones are formed and how to keep bones healthy. She was also able to talk about the qualities and attributes necessary for nursing using her technical expertise and the experiences of the children in the group who had been in hospital. Working collaboratively on a task, being able to discuss technical details and to use the information other children had provided allowed the able child to be challenged appropriately but also to feel part of the group discussion.

Working together on a task. As with play, some gifted and talented children would rather work alone than with someone else. While independent working should be encouraged, children must also learn to work together. Setting a task, such as a problem-solving task, and assigning key roles and tasks within the activity will allow adults to observe the kind of interaction that takes place. The assigning of roles and tasks means that all are clear about what is expected of them. The need to collaborate to achieve the outcome will result in children having to communicate with one another. Individual strengths can be utilised here. For example, if the children were to 'build an ambulance with doors that open', a child with good organisational skills can be responsible for gathering the necessary equipment; a child with good negotiating skills can be responsible for gathering the ideas for planning the design; a child with good motor development can be responsible for cutting out or manipulating the materials; a child with good communication skills can be responsible for reporting back to the wider group. Once secure in their roles, they can be encouraged to try out different roles. Gifted and talented children should also have the opportunity to work with intellectual peers. In other words, gifted and talented children should work on collaborative tasks with children who are operating at the same age intellectually. This may mean them working with children who are several years older than them in chronological terms. Working within and across age ranges will support highly able young children as they develop a sense of self and an understanding of their own abilities.

Interviews. Children who are confident and have advanced spoken language can be paired up with others (peers, adults, experts) and given the opportunity to interview them about a particular topic. Questions can be prepared in advance and the interviews can be recorded. This kind of activity allows for a variety of skills to be developed, including: questioning techniques, spoken language development, ICT skills, editing skills.

5 Being able to articulate thoughts and feelings is an important part of language development. We need to develop skills that allow us to think in difficult and abstract ways. We can do this by the following means:

- Using 'what if' questions allows already articulate children to explore things from a different perspective.

- Work with the children to gather and develop their ideas and the information they have acquired. What else can they find out? What are they going to do with the knowledge now? How else can they express that information and knowledge, e.g. through art, music, creative movement, drama, animation, science experiments?

- Set up 'what do we know?' times when children share information about particular topics. This allows the gifted and talented child to see that the information they have is valuable and contributes to the bigger pool of knowledge.

Listening/watching

Resources: Story CDs, books, songs

Activity/resources	Advanced responses	Challenging activities
Listening to instructions	• listens intently • can repeat back instructions • can remember a number of sequential instructions	1. increase complexity of instruction
Listening to stories	• listens intently • can answer questions about the story • can ask questions about the story • focuses on the task • becomes oblivious to everything round about	2. reading for meaning 3. 'feeling' detectives
Listening to peers and adults	• answers questions being asked • looks at their peers when they are talking • listens intently to adults and contributes to the discussion	4. responding to others 5. listening in a group
Watching	• looks for detail • asks higher-order questions, e.g. why have the other children upset the boy in the picture?	6. specific observations

1   Children can be given increasingly complex instructions. Adjectives can be added and directional language can be included. For example:

   • Go to the large red cupboard and open the door. On the second top shelf, underneath the boxes of jigsaws you will find the paintbrushes. Can you bring the paintbrushes to me?

2   Asking questions about a text allows the child to understand the text and to apportion meaning to it. Gifted and talented children often have a heightened sense in relation to feelings and empathy and they often have a well-developed awareness of justice and injustice. Offering children opportunities to ask questions about stories and characters that address these important issues in life allows children to feel they have explored difficult questions in a safe and secure environment. Adults should:

   • re-read the text so children can relate to the story

   • create opportunities to identify favourite stories and characters

   • create opportunities for talking

   • not be afraid to tackle difficult life issues head-on.

Non-fiction books should also be used in the same way. Using a variety of sources to gather information allows for in-depth discussions about how information is communicated. For example, newspapers, websites, encyclopedias, news bulletins are all useful sources of materials.

3   Children can be encouraged to listen for and identify words in the story or poem that are about feelings, such as:

- sad

- happy

- cry

- angry

- scream

- hug

- kiss

- smile.

Having identified them, discussion can take place about how we convey these feelings and emotions to others. Children should also be encouraged to listen to poetry and stories so that the rhythm and pattern wash over them. Listening with their eyes closed allows them to imagine the scenes depicted through the words.

4   Children need to learn to communicate and respond to others. Young children often find this hard and it is easier to lash out at someone than to reason and negotiate with them. The development of this area is inextricably linked with social and emotional development. Listening to others and responding appropriately takes time and practice. Children need to:

- read the other child's face, i.e. read the signs. Do they look happy? Do they look angry?

- see the other child's point of view; for example, if I take the crayon it will make him unhappy.

Cards with faces on them can be made. The children can help to select faces and stick them onto cards. They can also draw faces representing various emotions. This helps the children to think about facial features – e.g. screwed-up eyes when angry, wide-open eyes when smiling, etc. This can be related to activity 3 above. Helping children to recognise emotions and to recognise that behaviour is related to emotions will help the gifted and talented child to react more appropriately. For example, we need to help children realise that they hit the child because they were feeling angry. Connecting feelings to behaviour can be a powerful experience for children. Articulate gifted and talented children will often understand this relationship and be able, with support, to verbalise their feelings. Gifted and talented children also need support in 'reading' others and in understanding how to communicate their thoughts and ideas to them. Again the adult has a crucial role to play here. The adult can be the bridge between both the gifted child and their peers as they struggle to understand each other by:

- simplifying language as necessary

- linking what age peers say in response to the gifted child's comments and vice versa

- asking questions to move the conversation on

- making connections between conversations when it is clear that the children are not doing this for themselves.

5   Group situations do not reflect the flow of natural conversations. However, group discussion times do offer an opportunity to develop turn-taking. If children are reporting back on their work, telling a story or offering a point of view, then able children can be encouraged to ask questions arising from the details being given.

6   Observant children can be asked to look for a specific point in a picture or a story. For example:

- How does the digger get across the bridge?

- In what ways is the blue house different from the red one?

They can also be asked to connect what they see in one picture to another situation.

Children should be encouraged to look for detail and make connections across curricular areas. They can also be asked to hypothesise on future events or outcomes.

Writing

Resources: Paper, crayons, pencils, pens, chalk, chalkboards, charcoal, electronic resources, general mark-making materials

Activity/resources	Advanced responses	Challenging activities
Imaginative play, e.g. in the café/shop; travel agent's; vet's; hospital; etc.	• connects the marks they make with real-life situations • actively seeks out opportunities to 'practise' writing	1. offer real-life opportunities
'Have a go' writing table	• enjoys making marks – real or pretend • can tell you what the 'writing' says	2. use a variety of writing materials 3. advice and guidance on the formation of letters

Activity/resources	Advanced responses	Challenging activities
	• has a go at producing actual letters and numbers • grips the writing implement correctly • understands that groups of letters have meaning • asks 'how do you write...?'	4 computer work
Tracing and following patterns	• stays on the lines • selects an appropriate starting point and completes the task systematically • good hand–eye coordination • starts at the beginning and progresses logically	5 more intricate patterns 6 picture closure

1   As an extension to the child's eagerness to make meaningful marks a variety of situations can be created that incorporate the need to 'write'. For example:

   • the café – orders, till receipts, menus, signs

   • the shop – shopping lists, special offers, till receipts, credit card transactions

   • the travel agent's – details of holidays, client details

   • the hospital – recording of temperatures, case notes, prescriptions, patients' details

   • the vet's – pet's details, case notes.

If any parents or adults in the community can be involved in these role-play situations then they should be encouraged to work alongside the children, adding a further dimension to the 'real-life' approach. Interacting with adults in this way:

   • allows the children to hear a wider vocabulary related to the area

   • offers them an opportunity to see real-life examples of how to deal with and record situations

   • allows adults with expert knowledge to develop the skills and abilities the child may present.

2   A variety of writing implements should be on offer to the children. Some gifted and talented children do not like to work with lead pencils because of the texture and sound they make, so early years settings should ensure that they offer a variety of mark-making tools, including:

   • felt pens

   • calligraphy pens

- brush felt pens

- large bulbous ballpoint pens

- artists' pencils

- joiners' pencils

- gel pens

- charcoal

- wax crayons

- chalks

- biro pens

- coloured pencils.

Remember that the aim here is to encourage and develop the interest in writing. The focus should be on flow and rhythmic writing style, not on spelling and letter formation, although this will come later.

3   When children are showing an interest in forming letters adults can help and support them in this by:

- introducing them to the formation of letters in, for example, their name

- using sand in a tray for practising letter formation. The tactile approach works well for some children and a shake of the tray means mistakes are easily wiped out

- making sandpaper letters to promote letter formation as children can 'feel' the shape of a letter. Doing this with their eyes closed can also help them to 'see' the shape of the letter in their head

- introducing sets of letters which build up phonological awareness

- writing captions for display work.

Engaging the able child in discussion about the above activities allows the child to make connections between the marks and meanings. Adults can also model writing for the child when writing captions.

4   It is important to remember that writing for meaning does not only happen when we use a pencil and paper. Children should be encouraged to experiment with ICT to produce labels, captions and stories. Gifted and talented children can use programs such as Clicker Five to 'write' their own story. Those with a good grasp of letters can begin to investigate using the keyboard. The idea of the permanency of writing can be explored. They can save their work and return to it, amend it or add to it as necessary.

5   As the child's fine motor skills develop, more intricate patterns can be introduced. Curls, twists and loops all create an added challenge for the child.

Children can also be encouraged to use whiteboards and dry pens to develop gross motor and writing skills.

6   Picture or letter closure can be introduced. Children have to follow or trace the lines of a shape or object but have the added challenge of completing the picture or letter where the lines are missing.

Staff should consider how and where they set up writing activities. They should be in a comfortable place and tables should be an appropriate height for the age of child.

Reading

Resources: Books – fiction and non-fiction – leaflets, environmental print, e.g. notices, labels, computer

Activity/resources	Advanced responses	Challenging activities
In the library corner	• can be regularly found in the library corner • selects a book and gives reasons for doing so, e.g. 'I like the cover'; 'I've read about this character before' • selects a book and studies it in detail • listens and engages in the activity	1. access to a range of books in varying styles and genres 2. access to poetry books 3. access to non-fiction books 4. book reviews
Retelling a story using a book	• can retell the story accurately • can retell the story using phrases from the book • turns pages at appropriate point • can read 'between the lines'	5. offer opportunities for the children to engage in story-telling to the group 6. ask children to make up alternative endings to the story 7. build a picture from the text 8. draw a character using information from the text
Handling a book	• knows how to hold a book • knows about technical details, e.g. cover, title, author, etc. • knows where the story starts • knows how to turn pages • can follow text from left to right • looks after books	9. examine different kinds of literature 10. explore literature in a different language

(Continued)

(Continued)

Activity/resources	Advanced responses	Challenging activities
Environmental print	• asks what notices round the room say • attempts to 'read' the notices using clues to predict text • keen that notices round the room should be obeyed, e.g. 'only 4 at the sand'	11 have the children help make the signs for the early years setting 12 have the children make up their own signs and notices – link to topic work 13 walk round the catchment area looking for environmental print 14 discuss new words 15 collect new words

1 Ensure that there is a range of books that lead the children into reading 'chapter books'. Some books to look out for include:

- 'Go Bananas' series by Egmont Children's Books

- 'Red Fox Mini Treasures'. They include titles by Quentin Blake and Mairi Hedderwick, author of the Katie Morag books

- Roald Dahl's books, such as *The Enormous Crocodile* and *The Magic Finger*

- Emily Gravett's books, e.g. *Meerkat Mail*

- Oliver Jeffers's books, e.g. *Lost and Found*.

These are tried-and-tested stories that most children find irresistible.

2 Young children often love poetry. They love the rhyming words, the rhythm of poetry and they often particularly like nonsense poetry. Ensure that poetry books are a part of the library corner. These can be read by the children themselves or as part of 'story time'.

3 Ask the children to identify areas of particular interest and offer books on these areas. Usborne and Dorling Kindersley titles are particularly useful here. Children should be encouraged to bring books from home or the library if they have a particular interest.

4 Tell the children you are thinking about adding a particular book to the library. Ask the children to review the book for you and decide if it should be included or not. This not only develops their reading skills but their reporting and reasoning skills too and it will increase their self-confidence as they realise their views are being sought and listened to.

5 Ask children to retell a story to a group of their peers. They can do this using the book or by retelling the story in their own words. They could also pre-record the story and let other children listen to it. Story-telling in front of their peers allows children to develop a sense of audience and offers opportunities to develop expression, volume and voice projection.

6 Children can be asked to retell a well-known story but they have to provide an alternative ending. For example, tell the story of Jack and the Beanstalk but imagine the giant had been a kind, friendly giant instead of an angry, bad-tempered giant.

7 Encourage the children to see the 'picture' the author was trying to create. Ask them to tell you the words that build up this picture.

8 From reading a text, ask the children to paint, draw or create a character from the story using only the clues in the story to help them create the picture.

9 Have the children collect different kinds of literature, e.g. leaflets from the supermarket, museums, magazines, comics. Once they have a good collection of literature they can be encouraged to examine each kind of book, booklet, etc., and be asked to compare these with the books they have been reading and look for a comparison between:

   • the style

   • the layout

   • the pictures

   • the amount of writing

   • the thickness

   • the number of pages.

10 Literature from different cultures can be examined. For example, Arabic script can be discussed and the differences in how we read it explored – we read from right to left in Arabic. If you have staff or families who are Arabic speakers in your early years setting, they can be invited to talk to the children about their language and reading materials.

11 We know that involving children in rule-making means they are more likely to adhere to the rules. Having young children help to make up rules and accompanying signs can be a good way for educators to engage the children in discussion and helps to foster a sense of belonging. Children will also be able to decide what signage is required so that visitors can find their way around the early years setting. They can choose how best to produce the signs, e.g. on computer, handwritten and laminated, child's drawing, etc. Children can interview visitors to find out what signage is required. Discussions can also take place as to the height at which signs should be displayed – signs for children will have to be placed at a lower height than signs for adults. Older children or adults can be invited in to 'follow the signs'. Can they identify key areas of the early years establishment? For example:

   • the play area

   • the toilets

- the office

- the equipment cupboard

- the gym hall

- the music room

- the staffroom

- the headteacher's office.

12 Children can be encouraged to make up their own signs for topic work they are doing. The children could research 'real-life' signs for the topic area and then invent their own. For example, they could investigate road signs if they were studying 'my street'.

13 Children can go on an excursion outside of the early years setting to explore what kind of environmental print is around them. This can be done over a period of time and different groups can be taken to different areas so that a bank of signs is built up. Digital photographs can be taken on these excursions and a log can be built up showing key signs and aspects of environmental print in the local area. Visits could be made to:

- the park

- the supermarket

- the town centre

- the village hall

- look at road signs

- the hospital

- the vet's

- religious buildings.

14 Discuss how children learn 'new words'. Find out how they remember new words – do they look and remember, sound the word out, or remember the shape of the word if the word cannot be sounded out?

15 Children can collect 'new words' and build up a word bank. These words can be classified under headings, e.g. words from the living room:

- chair

- television

- rug

- carpet

- settee

- curtains.

Alternatively, you could use subject areas to categorise words, e.g. words we use in music:

- rhythm

- beat

- tune

- melody

- notes

- instruments.

Staff should think about how and where they organise reading experiences. Books should be easily accessible and the area for reading should be comfortable. Sometimes this will mean providing soft seating and at other times it might be more appropriate to sit at a table. Books should not just be confined to the book corner but should be found in all areas of the setting. **Remember:** a high reading age will have implications not only for reading but for other areas of the curriculum.

Moving Image Education – taking account of the 21st century

Moving Image Education (MIE) developed from the recognition that moving images in the form of film, cartoons, TV, etc. dominate our world. As suggested in Chapter 3, this means that when we think about literacy we need to think beyond the traditional ideas of the written and spoken word. Using moving images as the text children can discuss and analyse just as they would with the written word. Traditionally educators and parents have been concerned at the impact of film and the internet on young children. However, if we are to develop citizens for the 21st century we have to acknowledge that the world they will inhabit will consist of moving images. Through MIE children will develop skills associated with traditional literacy development. In other words the aim is the same – we want to help children to become literate – but the sources of the texts used might be different.

Some of the techniques used are certainly not new. For example, after some significant event, e.g. a natural disaster, a celebration, etc., educators might gather reports about the event from a variety of sources. Different newspaper articles can be collected and examined. The use of different writing styles aimed at different audiences can be discussed. Adding moving images to the collection of materials expands the sources and allows for wider comparisons. Accessing worldwide TV reports of the event can let children see how the event is reported in different countries. Whatever form the information is presented in children are still learning to analyse, present their views, interpret what they see/read, listen to other viewpoints and justify their views. We still want children to be confident, able to work with others and engaged in their learning. MIE assists us in this quest and is a useful tool for the early years practitioner as he/she seeks to support young children in literacy development. The website link given in 'Useful websites' below will allow you to access archived materials and a rich source of media texts.

1 Puppets are a wonderful resource to develop language skills. Early years settings should have a range of puppets on hand for children to play and engage with. Children can also make their own puppets from socks, scrap material, paper bags, etc.

Puppets can be used to:

- explore feelings – their own and the puppets'

- talk through difficult situations

- discover alternative strategies for behaviour, turn-taking, etc.

2 Other languages can be introduced, such as Spanish, Urdu, Mandarin Chinese. Rhythm and pattern within these languages can be explored. Scripts for languages can be studied and practised. The idea of directionality can be investigated. For example, Egyptian hieroglyphs were written in either horizontal direction, other scripts, such as Arabic and Hebrew, are written right-to-left. Find out if children or families in your setting are fluent in other languages, have family members visit and work with children teaching them phrases and numbers.

3 What constitutes dialect will depend on where you come from. In the UK and the USA linguists take a slightly different stance on what constitutes dialect. However, pronunciation and different words for everyday objects are good sources of interest for gifted and talented children, and encouraging children to explore language in all its forms is to be nurtured. For example, the Shetland Islands to the north of Scotland have developed resources for the promotion of the Shetland dialect which has both Nordic and Scottish roots. Materials are available for use in nurseries and schools and lifelong learning. More information is available at: http://www.shetlanddialect.org.uk/learning

Links can be developed with nurseries and schools in areas where a particular dialect is spoken and online discussions can offer opportunity for practise. Nurseries could participate in joint projects.

4 Children can play word games such as word searches or word mazes and they can play commercially produced games such as Scrabble or Boggle.

5 Children can make up tongue twisters. These can be used by other children in the setting and recordings can be made of the children as they say them. They can be worked on over a period of time and collated into a book.

6 As for activity number 5 but this time using poetry as the stimulus. Different kinds of poems can be written, spoken and collated, e.g.:

(Continued)

(Continued)

- *acrostic:* certain letters, usually the first letter in each line, form a word or message when read in a sequence

- *couplet:* rhyming stanzas made up of two lines

- *free verse:* rhymed or unrhymed lines with no fixed metrical pattern

- *haiku:* a Japanese poem composed in the pattern of 5,7,5 morae, which are similar to syllables

- *limerick:* a short humorous poem of 5 lines

- *rhyme:* a rhyming poem with same or similar sounding words usually at the end of a line.

7   If a child is reading fluently then finding out their reading age can be helpful as it will help staff to select appropriate reading material and to plan learning activities that are appropriate to the child's ability. Staff do need to be careful that the content of selected books is appropriate for the chronological age of the child. Just because they can access the text does not mean that the content is age appropriate.

Many of these activities are adult-led. For an even richer learning experience ask the children to help you devise these.

Summing up

Some key points and suggestions have been made in this chapter in relation to challenging activities in the area of language. They include:

- the importance of developing and challenging the skills young children display in literacy.
- offering some activities to challenge young children in their learning.

Useful websites

Early Childhood Australia http://www.earlychildhoodaustralia.org.au/learning_and_teaching/early_childhood_literacy/ advocates the promotion of quality, social justice and equity in all issues relating to the education and care of children from birth to eight years. The website has links to useful activities and articles about early learning.

Emily Gravett: http://www.emilygravett.com/ Emily's website has numerous interactive activities that children will enjoy. Various games, along with interviews with Emily, will be of interest to budding authors and illustrators.

London Gifted and Talented: http://teachertools.londongt.org/ This website is packed full of useful information about gifted and talented education. In particular the Teacher Tools section has practical ideas for the classroom. 'What do you mean?' is a particularly useful activity for those interested in language.

Moving Image Education (MIE): http://www.movingimageeducation.org/ is about helping young people to question, analyse, explore and understand the meaning of what they're watching and hearing. A project in Scotland looked at how to develop MIE in education. The website contains a section for early years staff and offers access to free materials.

National Literacy Trust: http://www.literacytrust.org.uk/early_years provides information relating to early years provision and literacy, including news, research, events, policy, resources and further information about our work in this area.

Scottish Story Telling Centre: http://www.scottishstorytellingcentre.co.uk/education/scottish_storytelling_education.asp is a network of professional story-tellers available throughout the year to visit schools. The website also contains links to resources and materials. The 'Storyrich resources' section contains practical tips on telling stories as well as stories and games to be used. The early years starter pack is full of useful information for all early years workers.

Further reading

Moses, B. (2010) *Able Writers in Your School*. UK: Andrews.

White, H. (2005) *Developing Literacy Skills in the Early Years: a Practical Guide*. London: SAGE Publications.

Whitehead, M.R. (2010) *Language and Literacy in the Early Years 0–7* (4th edn). London: SAGE Publications.

Mathematics

This chapter will:

- Consider why it is important to develop and challenge the skills young children display in mathematics.
- Offer some activities to challenge young children in their learning.

Early years educators need to engender a love for mathematics among the young children in their care. To do this they need to create an atmosphere conducive to mathematical thinking. They can do this by:

- celebrating mathematical thinking that takes place in the setting

- displaying mathematical work that has been done in the setting

- talking with the children about mathematical concepts

- having high mathematical expectations of the children they are working with

- encouraging children to experiment with mathematical thinking

- valuing all aspects of mathematics, not just numerical competency

- allowing children to think about mathematics so they are not always using concrete materials.

The UK appears to be facing some difficulties with regards to mathematics. International comparisons suggest that our children are doing much worse than children in other countries. There are, of course, inherent difficulties with such comparisons – we are not comparing like with like to start with, and scant regard is paid to significant differences, for example, children in Europe and beyond often start formal schooling much later than in the UK. Nonetheless, low achievement in the area of mathematics is something that early educators should be concerned about, if for no other reason than that the creativity and interest in mathematics that young children bring to the early years setting has to be the starting point for turning around the 'I hate' and 'I'm no good at maths' mindsets so often prevalent in our education establishments and in society at large. Unfortunately, we often think of mathematics as computation, in other words adding, subtracting, multiplying and dividing and yet maths is so much more. Maths is exciting, creative and fun and can be found in all aspects of life.

Good practice in this area will:

- develop existing skills
- help children to transfer skills they already possess from one situation to another
- offer new mathematical opportunities
- help children of all abilities to work together
- help children to enjoy mathematics.

Challenging activities

Number

Activity/resources	Advanced responses	Challenging activities
Recognising numerals, e.g. in pictures, imaginative play, etc.	• recognises a range of numbers in various contexts • uses number names beyond 10 • responds to the mathematical thinking of others	1. oral work
Counting, e.g. number of currants on buns	• counts accurately • counts reliably up to 10 and beyond	2. developing the language of number 3. counting on and counting back 4. developing number beyond 10 5. estimating
Talking about adding on, taking away etc.	• understands the concept of adding and subtracting • understands the concept of addition/subtraction in the abstract • can apply the concept within everyday situations, e.g. how many more cups do we need for snack time if there are 9 people in our group? • recognises the symbols for adding and subtracting	6. mental maths 7. real-life activities to enhance knowledge

1   Oral work should be an integral part of mathematical work in the early years setting. Opportunities should be provided for counting items. Number cards can be used to label items so that children are secure in matching a number to the name and can do this both orally and symbolically.

2   It is important that children understand and can use the language of number. Again, oral work will be useful here as the adult establishes and challenges the language of number – one more than, one less than, higher than, lower than, greater than, smaller than. Mathematical games can be useful here: not just the playing of games but also the creating of games. For example, children can use the idea of 'snakes and ladders' to make up their own game. This involves not just mathematics but also art work, discussion, the establishing of rules and interaction between the inventor of the game and their peers as they play with the finished product.

3   Children should be offered opportunities to count on and count back from any number. Any kind of numerical representations that are commonly found in the early years setting can help here such as:

-   a number line

-   a clock

-   number ladders.

Children should also be introduced to numbers in both vertical and horizontal positions.

It is also useful to think about how we lay out concrete items for counting. For example, when counting on you could:

-   Lay out three lions' heads in a triangular shape.

Add another two lion's heads.

-   How many heads altogether?

The layout will encourage children to count on: 3... 4, 5. Children should be encouraged to think about the various ways we can arrange items so that we can count on.

4   Able children will often be able to count well beyond 10. Where there is secure recognition of number names and digits, we can begin to develop the concept of tens and units. Children can be asked to collect and group objects into groups of 10.

These should be placed in the left hoop. The remaining objects should be placed in the right hoop.

5   An important part of this work is encouraging children to 'estimate'. This can be done by:

• presenting children with shapes such as:

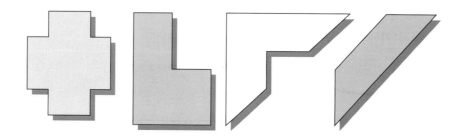

• asking the children to guess how many squared coloured tiles it will take to cover the shape

• asking the children to cover and count the shapes to see how close their estimation is.

This work also relates to area.

6   While the ability to do computation is often seen as an indicator of mathematical ability, it is argued that often young gifted mathematicians are far more interested in patterns, for example. We should therefore be wary of regarding

children to start the more formal aspects of addition and subtraction as a way of challenging children. In addition we should offer them:

- opportunities for engaging in 'real-life' mental mathematics; for example, calculating something for the early years setting – we have 23 children, 4 are staying for lunch; how many are going home?

- activities that involve adding on or taking away certain items. For example, I have 4 rings and 10 people. I want 3 people to stand in each ring. Do I have enough people? If not, how many more people do I need?

- opportunities to link adding on and taking away to other mathematical concepts such as money

- opportunities to explore the language of number through talking about, for example, 'half of...', 'double...', 'equal share of...'.

Shape, position, movement and patterns

Resources: Jigsaws, puzzles

Activity/resources	Advanced responses	Challenging activities
Jigsaws, puzzles	<ul><li>manipulates jigsaw pieces</li><li>can connect shape/colour of piece to shape/colour of space</li><li>knows what the final picture will be like</li><li>approaches the task logically, e.g. completes the corners first</li><li>connects the pieces with speed and ease</li></ul>	1. creating puzzles 2. Floor Turtles and Roamers
Identifying shapes	<ul><li>can name 2D and 3D shapes accurately</li><li>makes reference to properties of 2D and 3D shapes</li></ul>	3. further work on properties
Patterns and sequences	<ul><li>continues patterns</li><li>orally describes pattern</li><li>copies pattern accurately</li></ul>	4. life patterns and visualisation 5. Fibonacci numbers

One obvious way to challenge children in this area is to give them more complex puzzles and jigsaws, e.g. with a greater number of pieces, physically smaller pieces, no picture to copy, turn the jigsaw pieces over so shape is the only clue, etc. Some gifted and talented children can already complete 300-piece jigsaws at age three and so settings should ensure they have a range of puzzles, including 3D puzzles. Combining two or more jigsaws' pieces together can add challenge and mean that the children have to complete more than one puzzle at a time. Use established puzzle games such as The Tower of Hanoi to offer challenge. Another way to challenge the children is to have them make a jigsaw or puzzle themselves for their peers to use. This can be done in several ways:

- Give the children a blank piece of paper and ask them to cut it into different shapes and then piece it together again.

- Give the children a blank piece of paper and ask them to cut it into a particular number of different shapes and then piece it together again.

- Give the children a blank piece of paper and ask them to cut it into a particular number of pieces and in particular shapes; e.g. 12 pieces – four squares, four triangles and four rectangles – and then piece it together again.

- The above can be repeated but first the children can draw a picture on the paper before cutting it or print out a picture they have taken and make it into a jigsaw.

2 The use of Floor Turtles and Roamers can offer children opportunities to explore and experiment with shape, position and movement. Children can link this work to topic work being done in the early years setting. For example, if you are doing work on the hospital, children can:

- make the Floor Turtle or Roamer into an ambulance

- build a hospital from junk material

- create an 'incident' which results in people needing to be taken to hospital

- programme the Floor Turtle or Roamer to take the quickest route from the 'incident' to the hospital.

If you are working on 'myself' and the children live close to the early years setting, the children could:

- get the Floor Turtle or Roamer ready to go to the early years setting

- build a model of the early years setting

- build a model of their own houses

- plan routes from the house to the early years setting – features such as the swing park, the shops, granny's house can be added and will allow for a variety of routes to be developed and explored.

3 Children can:

- specify properties of shapes such as edges, corners, faces

- play with the shapes to see which roll, slide, etc.

- explore the faces of the shapes; for example, all the faces of a cube are the same; there are two triangles and three rectangles in a triangular prism

- look for 2D and 3D shapes in the world

- experiment through junk modelling

- make tiling patterns

- investigate 3D shapes and nets.

4   Often children in the early years are asked to 'copy patterns'. This usually involves coloured beads and cubes. Given that mathematicians argue that mathematics is all about patterns and sequences, the early years educator must widen his/her definition to include the kind of activities that foster a love of patterns and sequences. We need to allow children to explore life patterns such as:

- the seasons

- daily patterns

- weekly patterns

- yearly patterns.

Other patterns occur and should be considered, such as:

- musical patterns

- patterns in nature

- patterns in fabrics such as knitting, tweed, etc.

These kinds of patterns are often of much more interest to young able children and allow them to start to connect patterns with life around them. They will begin to see patterns everywhere and be keen to identify them and tell you about them. Telling you about the patterns and connections they can see will encourage children to start thinking like a mathematician. Visualising and creating mental images are an important part of mathematical thinking. Jennifer Piggot and Liz Woodham (2009) contend that when we solve problems we visualise in order to develop ideas and understanding. They argue that visualisation has three purposes:

1   To help children understand the problem.

2   To help children to see the problem.

3   To help children visualise possible solutions.

You can read more about this by going to the Nrich website http://nrich.maths. org/6447

5   Building on the idea of patterns, the Fibonacci numbers can be explored. The Fibonacci numbers were originally defined by the Italian mathematician Fibonacci, also known as Leonardo da Pisa, in the 13th century. The table below shows how they can be used when thinking about how many ways you can pay a given amount using only 1p and 2p coins (UK currency).

1p	2p	3p	4p	5p
1p	2p	1p+2p	2p+2p	1p+2p+2p
	1p+1p	2p+1p	1p+1p+2p	2p+1p+2p
		1p+1p+1p	1p+2p+1p	2p+2p+1p
			2p+1p+1p	1p+1p+1p+2p
			1p+1p+1p+1p	1p+1p+2p+1p
				1p+2p+1p+1p
				2p+1p+1p+1p
				1p+1p+1p+1p+1p
1 way	2 ways	3 ways	5 ways	8 ways

Information handling

Resources: Matrices, tree diagrams, the café

Activity/resources	Advanced responses	Challenging activities
Sorting	• looks for imaginative ways of completing the task • offers more than one solution • offers more than one criterion for selection	1. sorting and connecting
Matrices and tree diagrams	• can sort on a matrix using two or more criteria • able to identify own criteria for sorting • will record orders accurately in the café using own notation or making use of prepared charts or grids	2. interpreting data

1   As with patterns and sequences, sorting is often taken to mean 'sorting items', such as modes of transport, into categories. Sorting has to be viewed within the broader mathematical framework if it is to be useful. Therefore, sorting is closely related to sequences, patterns and relationships. Encouraging the gifted and talented to explore, examine and explain these relationships through sorting real-life examples will be beneficial to the child and the development of their mathematical thinking. Therefore the adult must encourage children to:

- identify characteristics of living things

- identify characteristics of items

- identify characteristics in the natural world

- examine the similarities between the identified characteristics

- examine the differences between the identified characteristics

- examine the changes that occur between the identified characteristics.

2　Interpreting information is an important aspect of mathematical thinking. Gifted and talented children may interpret results differently as they are thinking differently about a situation. They can connect already known facts to the new information in order to come to a new understanding. They can also 'invent' symbols to represent meaning. For example, they may invent a symbol for prices in the café. When the meaning of this symbol is explained to all, it becomes the accepted symbol for prices in the café.

Building up simple graphs from information collected by the children offers opportunities for the adult to explore how children are interpreting data. It also offers opportunities to gauge how and if they are connecting this to other mathematical concepts. You could:

- find out what each child has for breakfast

- make a block graph to represent this (vertical or horizontal)

- have numerals marked on the graph but do not include details of the foods

- ask children questions about the graph.

Supply the following information about the graph:

1　The same number of people eat Shreddies as Coco Pops.

2　Only one person eats Weetabix.

3　There are twice as many people who eat Cornflakes as Rice Krispies.

4　There are two less people who eat Sugar Puffs than toast.

When working with a child at first you may not be able to start with such complicated questions. However, mathematically able children will enjoy the challenge and will soon relish the opportunity to solve the puzzle and to make up their own questions.

What we eat for breakfast

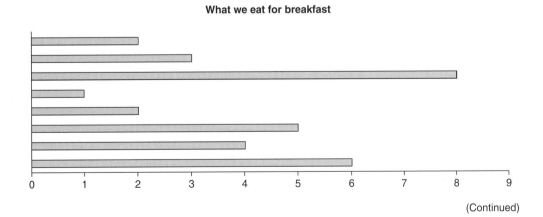

(Continued)

(Continued)

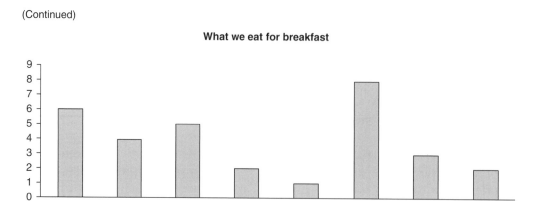

What we eat for breakfast

Money and measure

Resources: The café, the shop, coins, songs, rhymes, rods, rulers, height charts

Activity/resources	Advanced responses	Challenging activities
Handling money in the shop/café/travel agent's	• understands coins have different values • can identify different coins	1. equivalent values 2. currency
Non-standard units of measurement	• measures accurately • has grasped the importance of measuring accurately • is willing to estimate • estimates are reasonably accurate • has an understanding of the comparative nature of measure • uses the language of measure appropriately	3. real-life measuring experiences

1   Adults must not forget that different children may well have different understandings of money depending on their life circumstances. 'Saving up your pennies' will have a different meaning for a family for whom 'every penny counts' than for a child who is saving up for their second holiday abroad this year. However, equivalent values of coins will challenge the able child. Adults can ask:

   • How many different ways can you find of making 10p?

   • How many 1p make up 5p?

   • How many 50p make £1?

2   Exploring other currencies will allow the able child to:

   • know the names of different coins

   • relate coins to countries

- compare the images on the coins

- compare the shape of coins

- compare the thickness of coins.

This work links particularly well with the travel agent's activity. Children's experiences of travelling abroad for family visits or holidays will also bring this to life and will reaffirm the importance of culture for the young child. These kinds of activities develop the language of mathematics and help to explore mathematical concepts.

3   Measurement may involve:

- volume

- length

- height

- width

- capacity

- time

- mass.

It is believed that children's understanding of each of these will develop at different rates, but each is closely linked to real-life experiences.

Children can:

- engage in comparative measures; for example they can measure the table with cubes and with hand spans and then compare

- play games involving distance, such as hopscotch, to find out how and why people measure: do all containers hold the same amount of bricks?

- investigate the capacity of various containers in the sand and water

- use a timer when playing on the computer.

Whatever the activities, adults should have high expectations for mathematical development. This will involve opportunities for children to take risks and possibly get things wrong as they explore and develop their understanding of mathematics. This is particularly important as young children often want to please the adults around them and so it will be essential not to suggest that getting things right is what matters. For some gifted and talented young children learning from failure is crucial, especially if they consistently strive for perfection. Supporting young children to problem solve, to problem find, to discover that there is more than one right answer and more than one way of finding an answer will go some way to help them to build up resilience. Mathematics is yet another area that lends itself to cross-curricular work. Acknowledging that mathematics is much wider than computation and making sure that children experience mathematics in everyday situations will allow children to see maths in action.

---

1 Early years settings could begin to see mathematical concepts in much of their everyday work. Once adults adopt this broad and real-life approach to mathematics, they can more easily include activities that foster mathematical thinking. For example:

- making a bus that will hold 10 children

- growing seeds and seeing whose grows most

- buying cakes for the early years fair

- organising the jigsaws so they all fit on the shelf

- speculating why the short, fat jug holds more milk than the tall, thin jug

- working out how many minutes it is until lunch

- leaving out construction toys, squared paper, mazes, compare bears, logiboards and pegboards and discussing mathematical concepts as a result of how the children engage with the resources.

2 Gifted and talented children can further explore Fibonacci numbers and the Golden Ratio. This work links well to children's interest in patterns and in nature. They may also be interested in finding out more about Fibonacci himself and other well-known mathematicians such as the French mathematician, Blaise Pascal.

Many of these activities are adult-led. For an even richer learning experience ask the children to help you devise these.

Summing up

Some key points and suggestions have been made in this chapter in relation to challenging activities in the area of mathematics. They include:

- the importance of developing and challenging the skills young children display in mathematics
- the importance of developing mathematical thinking
- some activities to challenge young children in their learning.

Useful websites

BEAM (Be a mathematician): http://www.beam.co.uk/ promotes the teaching and learning of mathematics as interesting, challenging and enjoyable. The site contains, among other things, free resources for you to download.

Interactive maths games and activities: http://www.woodlands-junior.kent.sch.uk/maths/index.html This page has been developed by a primary school in England and links to a number of useful websites for mathematics.

Mathematical Magic of the Fibonacci Numbers: http://www.maths.surrey.ac.uk/hosted-sites/R.Knott/Fibonacci/fibpuzzles.html This website has some simple puzzles for children to consider.

Nrich: http://nrich.maths.org/public/ NRICH is a team of qualified teachers who are also practitioners in RICH mathematical thinking. The website offers free and interesting mathematical games, problems and articles for you and your children to use.

Primary resources: http://www.primaryresources.co.uk/ This site has free lesson plans, activity ideas and resources for primary teachers which can easily be adapted for early years.

Further reading

Koshy, V. (2002) *Teaching Young Gifted Children 4–7*. London: David Fulton.

Koshy, V. and Chester, M. (2007) *Mathematical Activities for Younger Gifted Children*. London: Elephas.

Piggott, J. and Pumfrey, L. (2007) *Maths Trails: Visualising*. Cambridge: Cambridge University Press.

Learning is fun and for all

In this chapter you will:

- **Consider why we owe it to our children to ensure they encounter challenging activities in the early years.**
- **Think about children who have 'double exceptionality'.**
- **Identify points for good practice.**
- **Think about how we can develop existing practice within early years.**

Threads of learning

If we look across the chapters in this book we can begin to see fine threads weaving their way through the content. These combined threads of attitude, belief, observation, identification and challenging activities allow us to make connections and to link together learning experiences. These learning experiences when considered as a whole will inform our decisions about learning:

- Is it something that excites me?

- Is it something I want to do more of?

- Is it something that I have control over?

- Is it something that I can contribute to?

Young children will be asking these questions as they engage in activities. Adults will also ponder these questions as they seek to develop practice. The developing of practice means that as adults we can influence how young children ultimately answer questions about learning. That's an exciting thought.

We know that young children want to learn. They are creative, receptive and motivated. The key is for educators to keep these sparks alive. This can be increasingly difficult in a culture that demands a more formal approach to learning earlier rather than later.

However, a failure to challenge gifted children, and indeed all children, may result in:

- underachievement

- challenging behaviour: acting-out behaviour or quiet, withdrawn behaviour

- boredom

- frustration

- an extinguishing of their natural love of learning

- a stifling of their creativity

- feelings of embarrassment in relation to their abilities

- an inability to relate to peers.

I have never met an early years educator who would want any of the above to be the end result for a child in their care. Therefore offering challenge to children becomes a 'must' rather than an 'add-on extra'.

The importance of the adult

Of key importance in the education of children are the adults in the early years setting. Adults have to:

- believe there are gifted and talented children in their early years setting

- be on the lookout for children who display particular abilities

- challenge children in their learning

- be ready to be surprised.

Early years educators need to be alert to the possibility that young gifted and talented learners may also have other labels attached to them. This is what Diane Montgomery (2003) calls 'double exceptionality' or multiple exceptionality. In other words, a child may have been identified as having, for example, attention deficit hyperactivity disorder (ADHD), but given the right opportunities the same child may be equally deserving of the label 'gifted and talented'. Some common 'double exceptionalities' include:

- autistic and gifted and talented

- Asperger and gifted and talented

- social, emotional and behavioural difficulties and gifted and talented

- ADHD and gifted and talented

- dyslexic and gifted and talented

- dyspraxic and gifted and talented

- English as additional language and gifted and talented.

One of the challenges for the educator is to see past that initial label and realise that behind it lies a child with unique abilities. Offering challenging learning opportunities will allow these children to emerge from behind that first label and with help and support show what they can achieve.

Developing good practice

Generic points for good practice for our work with gifted and talented children in the early years setting emerge from the previous chapters. While this is not an exhaustive list, it is a good starting point for the early years setting that is seeking to develop and enhance the abilities of gifted and talented children.

- Think about what intelligence means to you.
- Look at the child holistically, gather information from a variety of sources.
- Pull that information together and use it to inform planning.
- Observe children during activities.
- Plan to challenge the child who demonstrates advanced responses.
- Offer challenging opportunities that take account of what the child can already do. This should extend to every curricular area.
- Involve the child in their learning.
- Develop the whole child.
- Never put a 'glass ceiling' on a child and their abilities; help them to reach for the stars.

These points for good practice appear in a photocopiable sheet. This will allow your early years setting to identify areas of good practice and areas for development.

Working with young learners is a privilege and, in my experience, a source of constant amazement. They consistently surprise you with their:

- insight

- humour

- sense of wonder

- love of learning

- ability to absorb knowledge

- love of life.

Table 8.1 How are we doing?

Area for consideration	Work still to commence	Work in progress	Work well established	Comments
An agreed definition of intelligence				
Gathering information from a variety of sources				
Use of variety of information to inform planning				
Observation of children to identify advanced responses				
Design challenging actitivities for children displaying advanced responses				
Offer challenging activities for children displaying advanced responses				
Involving the child in their learning				
Developing the whole child				
No setting of artificial limits				

Harnessing these dispositions and channelling them towards challenging learning experiences will allow children to grow and develop.

Current trends likely to be found in early years and on which we can build include:

- Forest Schools

- Active Learning

- Aspects from Reggio Emilia, for example documenting children's learning

- Responsive planning

- Growing fruit and vegetables.

Much of the good practice in existence in early years settings already allows the needs of gifted and talented young children to be met but it is crucial that the adults in the setting have actively thought about gifted and talented children and planned accordingly.

For example, although the idea of Forest Schools originated in Scandinavia in the 1950s and outdoor learning has been valued for well over a century, Forest Schools have been springing up all over the UK in recent years. How might Forest Schools allow for high-end challenge?

Forest Schools

Learning outdoors is not a new concept and Forest Schools are building on the good work taking place in many settings across the UK. As the name suggests the learning ideally takes place in a forest or woodland area. Being in such an environment allows children to explore and find out about the world around them. Gifted and talented children can:

- set up experiments and investigate how nature works

- develop hypotheses

- test their hypotheses

- record their findings

- set up a similar experiment

- try to replicate their findings

- report their findings to a wider audience.

Such activities cross curricular boundaries and working as part of a group allows children to discover and develop particular interests and abilities. For example, one child might be interested in developing formats for recording results, another might find novel ways of sharing the findings with their peers. The beginnings of a scientific learning community will emerge and of course these skills can be brought back into the setting and transferred to other activities. Clearly all children can engage in such learning. What will mark this out for the gifted and talented child is the practitioner's acknowledgement of the child's advanced abilities and how this knowledge is then used to design activities, guide and advise during the activity, and shape the outcomes for individuals.

Task	All children	Gifted and talented child
Set up experiment and investigate how nature works	Set up experiment, e.g. collection of leaves in various stages of decay	Set up experiment, e.g. collection of leaves in various stages of decay
Develop hypothesis	Predict what they will look like on the next visit. Record (photograph, diagram)	Record (photograph, life-size diagram accurately measured, make a table and record properties in words) of what they look like. Predict what they will look like on the next visit. Give reasons for their prediction. Record their hypothesis (life-size diagram reflecting any predicted changes in measurement)
Test their hypothesis	Examine recorded data from previous trip and compare it to what they find	Examine recorded data from previous trip and compare it to what they find
Record their findings	Update records	Update records. Give reasons for the changes that have occurred. Indicate where their hypothesis was correct and why
Set up a similar experiment		Collect a new set of leaves or collect different materials e.g. twigs, berries, lichen, etc.
Try to replicate their findings		Repeat the stages above
Report their findings to a wider audience	Tell the rest of the group verbally and using the data they gathered what they have found	Tell the rest of the group verbally and using the data they gathered what they have found. Make a DVD of the findings. Record their findings in booklet form and build up the results of a number of experiments. Explain the new set of results and compare them to the original experiment – are they different? Why/why not?

These ideas use the stimulus of and opportunities offered by Forest Schools to allow for in-depth learning depending on the child's interests and abilities. However, learning opportunities like this can be created across the curriculum and in a variety of locations. Once again we can see that if the practitioner is actively thinking about high ability and challenge they can build in opportunities for gifted and talented learners.

Developing citizens for the 21st century

It is not enough to simply challenge the academic abilities a child displays. At the same time we have to acknowledge and take account of the important part emotions and feelings play in learning. If we are serious about developing citizens for the 21st century then we have to support children holistically as they grow and develop. In other words, we have to develop the whole child. Work in this area links well to the current focus on citizenship.

Working with children in a way that acknowledges:

- their range of abilities

- their interests

- their right to be involved in the planning of their learning

- their need to work collaboratively with others

- their need to think about how they learn

- their feelings

will not only challenge them academically but will challenge them emotionally as well. As a survivor of the holocaust said:

> Dear teacher
>
> I am a survivor of a concentration camp. My eyes saw what no man should witness: gas chambers built by learned engineers; children poisoned by educated physicians; infants killed by trained nurses; women and babies shot by high-school and college graduates.
>
> So I am suspicious of education.
>
> My request is: help your students to become more human. Your efforts must never produce learned monsters, skilled psychopaths, educated Eichmanns.
>
> Reading, writing and arithmetic are important only if they serve to make our children more human. (Oxfam, 2002: 17)

For some children, their families will offer exciting activities and be keen to develop their learning. For other families, the chore of living will be enough to cope with and any formal learning that takes place may almost appear incidental. It is therefore crucial that early years settings offer a wide range of opportunities to the children in their care. Geniuses may not start as child prodigies. Similarly, exceptionally able adults were often not recognised in the early years. Practice, encouragement from significant others and development over time all played their part in creating the person they came to be. Childhood is precious. Caring for and nurturing the children in our early years settings will offer them opportunities for development – academically and emotionally.

Not all children will be given the label 'gifted and talented'. But all children deserve to receive high-quality learning experiences that allow them to grow and develop in ways that they, and sometimes you, never thought possible.

Summing up

Some key points and suggestions have been made in this chapter. They include:

- considering why we owe it to our children to ensure they encounter challenging activities in the early years
- thinking about children who have 'double exceptionality'
- identifying points for good practice
- thinking about how we can develop existing practice within early years.

Useful websites

Forest Schools: http://www.forestschools.com/early-years-and-pre-school-forest-schools-case-study.php This website offers some early years case studies.

Oxfam Education: http://www.oxfam.org.uk/education/resources/category.htm?1 This website has downloadable activities for developing global citizenship.

Further reading

Knight, S. (2009) *Forest Schools and Outdoor Learning in the Early Years*. London: SAGE Publications.

Montgomery, D. (2003) *Gifted and Talented Children with Special Educational Needs*. London: David Fulton.

Glossary

Active learning – learning which engages and challenges children and young people's thinking using real-life and imaginary situations

Alternative model of assessment – understanding is arrived at by collaboration between the adult and the learner

Contextualised learning – learning within a real-life situation or context

Discrete approaches to thinking – using techniques, programmes and resources to encourage thinking

Double exceptionality – a child who has more than one label, e.g. 'dyslexia' and 'gifted and talented'

Entity theory of intelligence – believing a person possesses a specific amount of intelligence and nothing you or they can do will change that amount

Folk model of assessment – a set of beliefs about assessment that have grown and developed over the years

Forest Schools – outdoor learning, usually in a woodland, that encourages hands on, practical experiences

Goal achievement – performance goals are important; you have to show how clever you are

Holistic picture – gathering data from a variety of sources that allows the educator to build up a complete picture of the child and their learning

Hot-housing – pushing children on quickly through the stages of the formal curriculum

Inclusive education – children learning together: learning from each other, from adults around them and from their communities and families

Incremental theory of intelligence – believing that intelligence is not an 'entity' that resides within a person but is something that can be developed through learning

Infusion model of thinking – opportunities for thinking are built into the curriculum

Learning goals – becoming smarter is important to you and therefore learning is important

Mindset – a set of beliefs a person holds

Moving Image Education – using images as text children can discuss and analyse

Multiple exceptionality – a child who has more than one label

Multiple intelligences – A range of intelligences, as noted by Howard Gardner. They include musical, interpersonal, logical-mathematical, etc.

Participative learners – children who like to learn by copying a more knowledgeable other

Responsive planning – plans are developed with the child and respond to their interests

Standardised test – a test given to a group of pupils to gauge performance against either a national average (*norm-referenced*) or a breadth of subject material (*criterion-referenced*)

Tall poppies – children who are demonstrating abilities beyond what might be expected for their age

References

Ainscow, M. (1998) 'Would it work in theory? Arguments for practitioner research and theorising in the special needs field', in C. Clark, A. Dyson and A. Millward (eds) *Theorising Special Education*. London: Routledge.

Bloom, B.S. (1956) *Taxonomy of Educational Objectives: The Classification of Educational Goals. Handbook I: Cognitive Domain*. New York: McKay.

Bruner, J. (1996) *The Culture of Education*. Cambridge, MA: Harvard University Press.

Carr, M. (2001) *Assessment in Early Childhood Settings*. London: SAGE.

Collins (1988) *The Collins Concise English Dictionary*. London: Collins.

Colman, A.M. (1987) *Facts, Fallacies and Frauds in Psychology*. London: Routledge.

de Bono, E. (1976) *Teaching Thinking*. London: Penguin Books.

Department for Education and Skills (DfES) (1998) *Excellence for All Children: Meeting Special Educational Needs* (Green Paper). London: DfES.

Department for Education and Skills (DfES) (2001) *Special Educational Needs*. London: DfES.

Dweck. C. (1999) *Self Theories: Their Role in Motivation, Personality and Development*. Philadelphia, PA: Psychology Press.

Ennis, R.H. (1962) 'A concept of critical thinking', *Harvard Educational Review*, 32: 81–111.

Fisher, R. (1990) *Teaching Children to Think*. Oxford: Basil Blackwell.

Florian L. (2008) 'Special or inclusive education: future trends', *British Journal of Special Education*, 35(4): 202–208.

Gardner, H. (1983) *Frames of Mind*. London: Paladin.

George, D. (1997) *The Challenge of the Able Child* (2nd edn). London: David Fulton.

Gilhooly, K.J. (1996) *Thinking: Directed, Undirected and Creative*. London: Academic Press.

Gross, M.U.M. (1993) *Exceptionally Gifted Children*. London: Routledge.

Harrison, C. and Pound, L. (1996) 'Talking music: empowering children as musical communicators', *British Journal of Music Education*, 13(3): 233–242.

Koshy, V. and Casey, R. (1997) *Effective Provision for Able and Exceptionally Able Children*. London: Hodder and Stoughton.

Lenz Taguchi, H. (2010) 'Rethinking pedagogical practices in early childhood education: a multi-dimensional approach to learning and inclusion', in N. Yelland (ed.) *Contemporary Perspectives on Early Childhood Education*. London: Open University Press.

Lewis, J. (1998) 'Embracing the holistic/constuctivist paradigm and sidestepping the post-modern challenge', in C. Clark, A. Dyson and A. Millward (eds) *Theorising Special Education*. London: Routledge.

Lipman, M. (1991) *Thinking in Education.* Cambridge: Cambridge University Press.

McGuiness, C. (1999) *From Thinking Skills to Thinking Classrooms* (DfEE Research Brief 115). London: DfEE.

McLean, A. (2003) *The Motivated School.* London: Paul Chapman.

Malaguzzi, L. (1996) 'The right to environment', in Filippni, T. and Vecchi, V. (1996) *The Hundred Languages of Children: the Exhibit Reggio Emilia: Reggio Children.*

Mares, L. (1991) *Young Gifted Children.* Melbourne: Hawker Brownlow.

Mercer, N. (2000) *Words and Minds: How We Use Language to Think Together.* London: Routledge.

Ministy of Education (1995) Te Whāriki. Available at www.educate.ece.govt.nz (accessed August 2011).

Montgomery, D. (2003) *Gifted and Talented Children with Special Educational Needs.* London: David Fulton.

Oxfam (2002) *Global Citizenship: The Handbook for Primary Teaching.* Oxford: Oxfam.

Piggott, J. and Pumfrey, L. (2007) *Maths Trails: Visualising.* Cambridge: Cambridge University Press.

Piggott, J. and Woodham, L. (2009) *Thinking Through, and By Visualising Nrich.* Available at www.nrich.maths.org/6447. (accessed October 2011).

Poplin, M.S. (1988) 'The reductionistic fallacy in learning disabilities: replicating the past by reducing the present', *Journal of Learning Disabilities,* 21(7): 389–400.

Scottish Executive Education Department (SEED) (2003) *Moving Forward! Additional Support for Learning.* Edinburgh: HMSO.

Scottish Network for Able Pupils (2004) *Principles.* Available at: www.ablepupils.com (accessed 20 September 2011).

Scottish Office Education and Industry Department (SOEID) (1994) *Effective Provision for Special Educational Needs.* Edinburgh: HMSO.

Siraj-Blatchford, I. and Sylva, K. (2004) 'Researching pedagogy in English pre-schools', *British Educational Research Journal,* 30(5) 713–730.

Thurtle, V. (1997) 'Growth and development', in J. Taylor and M. Woods (eds) *Early Childhood Studies.* London: Arnold.

United Nations (1989) *Convention on the Rights of the Child.* UN General Assembly Document A/RES/44/25. New York: United Nations.

United Nations (1994) *Framework for Action.* Paris: UNESCO.

Wallace, B. (2002) *Teaching Thinking Skills Across the Early Years: A Practical Approach for Children Aged 4 to 7.* Slough: NFER.

Walsh, G., Murphy, P. and Dunbar, C. (2007) *Thinking Skills in the Early Years: A Guide for Practitioners.* (Written in collaboration with the Early Years Enriched Curriculum Evaluation Project Team.) Available as a PDF at: http://www.nicurriculum.org.uk/docs/skills_and_capabilities/foundation/ThinkingSkillsintheEarlyYears_Report.pdf (accessed September 2011).

Ziegler, A. (2005) 'The Actiotope Model of giftedness', in R.J. Sternberg and J.E. Davidson (eds) *Conceptions of Giftedness.* New York: Cambridge University Press.

Index